# Martial Arts Teaching Tales of Power and Paradox

## FREEING THE MIND, FOCUSING CHI, AND MASTERING THE SELF

**PASCAL FAULIOT**

TRANSLATED BY JON GRAHAM

Inner Traditions

Rochester, Vermont

Inner Traditions International
One Park Street
Rochester, Vermont 05767
www.InnerTraditions.com

First U.S. edition published by Inner Traditions 2000

Originally published in French in 1981 by Éditions Retz under the title *Les contes des arts martiaux* by Jean Markale

Copyright © 1981 by Éditions Retz; 1988 by Éditions Albin Michel S. A.
English translation copyright © 2000 by Inner Traditions International

Library of Congress Cataloging-in-Publication Data

Fauliot, Pascal.
    [Contes des arts martiaux. English]
    Martial arts teaching tales of power and paradox : freeing the mind,
    focusing chi, and mastering the self / by Pascal Fauliot ; translated by
    Jon Graham.—1st U.S. ed.
        p. cm.
    ISBN 0-89281-882-4 (alk. paper)
    1. Martial arts—Psychological aspects. 2. Martial arts—Philosophy.
3. Martial artists—Anecdotes. I. Title.

    GV1102. 7.P75 F38 2000
    796.8—dc21
                            00-025656

Printed and bound in Canada

10 9 8 7 6 5 4 3 2 1

Text design and layout by Priscilla Baker
This book was typeset in Adobe Caslon

Inner Traditions wishes to express its appreciation for assistance given by the government of France through the ministère de la Culture in the preparation of this translation.

Nous tenons à exprimer nos plus vifs remerciements au government de la France et le ministère de la Culture pour leur aide dans le préparation de cette traduction.

# Contents

# Preface

## Stories of Wondrous Wisdom and Dancing In Emptiness

*With one end of his bow*
*The archer pierces heaven.*
*With the other, he penetrates the earth.*
*Stretched between the two,*
*The bowstring hurls the arrow*
*Into the heart of both the visible and the*
*invisible target.*

### ZEN ARCHER'S MAXIM

It is always a pleasure to see a new book appear that teaches wisdom in a roundabout manner by means of poetry or tales. The Japanese tradition, like all authentic traditions, is extremely rich in stories and narratives of this kind; nor is the Buddhist tradition to be found wanting when it comes to supplying its own share of wondrous tales.

In choosing to assemble tales and narratives of the martial arts, Pascal Fauliot is of the opinion he has created a work of adaptation. We can view his selection of texts simply as an agreeable and pleasant anthology of events and tales, some of which are based on real life, as is the case with Eugen

Herrigel's memories of the great bow master Awa, or those concerning the founder of aikido, Master Ueshiba. But whether a tale be "real" or marvelous, it is difficult to know where history ends and story begins in the subtle and somewhat magical world of the great masters. It is obvious that the "ultimate secret" is never truly transmittable; nevertheless, one who wishes to grow in understanding, be initiated, or even "steal" the secret, can find a way, as in the case of the nineteenth-century story of young Yang Lu Chan, who successfully infiltrated the family of Master Chen Chang Hsiang, keeper of a secret form of barehanded combat, known from then on as tai chi. In this story, Yang, who had been hired as a servant, was caught secretly following the master's lessons. No one had ever before succeeded in stealing this centuries-old secret. Yang's eavesdropping even placed his life in danger. But the master saw that Yang's action was motivated by a genuine desire to learn. He completed the lesson and, subsequently, Yang in turn became a great master, partially due to his knowledge of the secrets of tai chi, the greatest of all martial arts traditions.

All of these stories contain teachings that allow us to see the rational mind ensnared, its desire for effectiveness at any cost caught in a trap of its own making. Another underlying reality of an almost absolute proficiency also appears, which is revealed in the failed attempts of certain individuals who, while attempting to act against or attack a master, are subtly defeated or stricken to the depths of their souls. One story depicts the ill fortune that befalls a pack of ruffians attacking a tai chi master, who apparently allowed their attack to proceed unhindered; another features the master Awa, who, wishing to demonstrate that once the essentials have been mastered, proficiency is supplied in abundance, plants an arrow in the center of a target at the back of a darkened corridor, then shoots another arrow that splits the first down the middle. In another, the agile strength of one ancient master pushes the ardent spirit of a young samurai to its limits. These examples can be infinitely multiplied. The objective of all these stories is to provide the realization that the threshold to be attained and the reality to be understood are not obvious, that true efficiency is most often secret, even intentionally hidden away, because the height of true wisdom is to make a game of it and pretend that one knows nothing. I have personally known several true masters who could easily be confused for the most ordinary of individuals. This custom is still alive and well, particularly in the world of Islamic Sufism. In fact, this being hidden in full sight has become one of the essential characteristics of Sufism. Very often it is said that a *pir*, a master, and even moreso the *qutub*, the "pole," the Master of masters, must remain unknown, often even to him- or herself. Humanity is widely seeded with individuals whose inner quality is a determinative force field that enhances and protects life. These individuals are spiritual focal points who exist to create the beneficial influences conducive to maintaining or transmitting a secret tradition.

The strength of the immutable, the comprehension of what is beyond time, the strength of the One included in the moving forms of thought, the free and centered power of a being who has liberated himself from fear and desire—these are some of the qualities that permit the mind to act freely and with the most sudden effectiveness. But these stories aren't told as illustrations of a gradual kind of training and its benefits, but as demonstrations of how every hour of the day should be faced with a certain clarity of consciousness. We see this idea expressed in numerous narratives, for example, in the story of Grand Master Toda Seigen confronting fencing champion Umedzu, which in turn recalls the battle Myamoto Musashi is forced to fight against the impetuous samurai, Sasaki. In both cases calm and self-mastery triumph, not over brute strength, because they are facing, after all, adversaries who themselves are masters, but a strength that has been imperfectly understood and mastered. This marks the appearance of that subtle spirit that is the secret of secrets: the further one descends (or climbs) in knowledge, the more obvious the importance of the infinitesimal becomes. It is that little something of no more weight than a glance or a thought, or even less, that is the essential source of all power. It is the discovery that the most refined quality is still never the ultimate quality; there is another existing beyond it, which is constantly hidden or veiled. The real combat takes place in this world of the infinitely subtle and inexpressible. When oneness is realized by a great master, it is emptiness itself that acts through him. The ego is effaced, but the strength of the universe, and the eternal movement of timeless, boundless cosmic power—a force impossible to name or even grasp with thought—acts in complete sovereignty.

This is the ultimate secret behind all the others. The stories and the marvels they relate tell us that individuals existed—and still exist—who understood these absolute principles and embodied them here on earth. No doubt everything is relative, and a great master can always find one greater. But he or she lives in a realm where competition has ceased and where there is no becoming because everything is. It is a stable point that exists in everyone and is well within the capability of all to realize, for it only requires something else that already exists within everyone as well: an opening to the infinite wisdom within, an opening that allows free wisdom to break forth and flower, which like that of these fascinating masters, is what is really behind all the gestures, finger movements, and little sticks associated with the martial arts. It is the reality that underlies even the most seemingly insignificant thing, the very dance of emptiness.

MICHEL RANDOM

# 1

## The Message of the Stories

The masters have always relied on the magic of storytelling to express the inexpressible. Thus, it is not surprising that stories from the martial arts tradition can convey the profound meaning of these disciplines that primarily constitute a school of life.

The most surprising aspect of the stories gathered in this book is that, for the most part, they are derived from actual events. This makes their impact all the more striking. They are proof positive that life masks a mystery, a secret we may hardly suspect. They give us a taste of an unknown dimension and attest to the fact that the incredible is not the impossible and that the extraordinary can merge with the events of everyday life.

Not being morality tales, these exemplary narratives have nothing to prove. Their goal is something different: to provoke questions whose only answers are found in experience and practice.

## THE ART OF STOPPING THE SPEAR

The true martial art should not be mistaken for a simple combat sport. A rudimentary sign or a symbol can often express what a long speech cannot. The ideograms designating the martial arts are identical in China and Japan; only the pronunciations are different. The Chinese say *wu shu,* the Japanese *bujutsu.* The translation "martial art," or the "art of combat," is a partial betrayal of the spirit of the original ideogram, which can be broken down into two characters meaning "to stop" and "spear." First conceived of as the "art of stopping the spear," the martial arts still derive much of their essential meaning from this original definition, all the more so since this formula can be interpreted simultaneously as the "art of stopping the spear of one's adversary" and the "art of stopping one's own spear." It is the great art of outer pacification and inner harmony.

## THE ART AND THE WAY

In ancient civilizations, whose remnants still flourish in the East, the traditional arts lead onto a path or way that allows people, at the cost of a long and arduous apprenticeship, to deepen their experience of reality and themselves. Little by little, the apprentice discovers the laws that govern the subtle forces with which life is woven, and he or she learns that the quality of one's work depends on whether one can master oneself, that is, master what he or she is. One's outer work becomes the prop of an inner metamorphosis.

This is the reason behind the confused notion of martial arts that lets us translate *kung fu* as simply "Chinese boxing." When speaking of their art of barehanded combat, the Chinese say *chuan shu*, "the art of the fist." Kung fu's actual meaning concerns the conscious and persistent effort and training one follows with an eye to realizing a work of art or achieving self-mastery. Thus the confusion that arises stems from the close relationship that exists in China between the martial arts and the self-realization of the individual. Far from being used exclusively for the art of combat, the term *kung fu* serves to express the level a person has reached in any field of activity. The Chinese will say of a calligrapher who has executed a quality work, that his kung fu is quite advanced.

In Japan there is the way of calligraphy *(shodo)*, the way of ceremony *(chado)*, the way of flower arrangement *(kado)*, in fact there is a way for each of the ancient arts. The art of combat is no exception: the *budo* designates the precipitous path that snakes through the heart of the martial arts. The way of combat is steep. The presence of an adversary demands self-presence in even the slightest gesture, thereby making it a matter of life and death. A break in concentration, a slight lag between the respective responses of mind and body will not be excused in actual combat and are not even without risk in training. One quickly discovers that the most dangerous adversary that can be found is oneself. The way of combat is thus endowed with a completely different meaning.

In Japanese the word *dojo* means "the place of the way." Here is where *budo* is practiced. Equivalent to a temple, the *dojo* is a sacred space in which a person receives a teaching, exercises, and finds revitalization. But *budo*, as has been said repeatedly by the masters, is not something that is practiced only at the *dojo*. It is the basis for an art of living tested at every moment.

The true *dojo*, add the masters, is the one the disciple builds within the depths of his own heart.

## THE GENESIS OF WU SHU

The origin of *wu shu*, Chinese martial arts, remains impossible to establish. The *chuan shu*, the art of barehanded combat, is the most renowned martial art of today. Its roots go back as far as the second millennium B.C. Pottery and frescoes dating from 1400 B.C. depict combat techniques that utilize the hands and feet. It seems that *chuan shu* became a complete discipline in its own right quite quickly, perhaps even from the outset, as is unquestionably shown by the postures found on a parchment coming from the Han Dynasty (202 B.C.). In addition to the martial and therapeutic techniques that are depicted, there is a symbolic and sacred vocabulary of gesture.

*Chuan shu* and Taoism, the Chinese initiatic path, have been intimately linked since the time of legends. There are countless traditions tracing the creation of a school of combat to a Taoist adept. This is confirmed by official history in the annals that preserve the memory of a famous Taoist physician who created a system based on the relationship between the behavior of five animals and the five elements of Chinese alchemy.

But the greatest place in legend is reserved for a Buddhist monk who transported a revolutionary system in his beggar's pouch.

## AT THE SCHOOL OF BODHIDHARMA

Tamo, better known under the name of Bodhidharma (the Enlightened One), was an Indian monk who traveled throughout China at the beginning of the sixth century A.D. in an effort to renew Buddhism, which had sunk into a state of total decadence. The reforming trend that he initiated took on the name of *chan,* which became *zen* in Japan.*

After having traveled for the greater part of his life, the

---

* Zen is based on the practice of the meditation posture in which Buddha achieved awakening. This is a straight, unmoving posture that consists of remaining seated with one's legs crossed in the lotus or half-lotus position, and keeping one's attention concentrated on long deep breaths pushed into the *hara,* also known as *kikai tanden*: the sea of energy that can be found three finger widths beneath the navel. One's thoughts, which pass like clouds in the sky, should not be heeded.

patriarch of Zen settled at the Shaolin monastery. Ascertaining on his arrival how incapable the monks there were of reaching the levels of concentration necessary for meditation, he was not long in discovering the cause. They were weakened by ascetic exercises, endless doctrinal discussions, and most important, they had abandoned all physical exercise. In order to restore their health and allow for the harmonious union of body and mind, in his opinion the source of all spiritual evolution, Bodhidharma taught the monks movements that had originated for the most part in Indian and Chinese martial arts, which he had perfected over the course of his long and perilous journeys. This method, topped off with techniques borrowed from hatha-yoga, took on the name of I Chin Ching.

The monastery of Shaolin subsequently became the most renowned school of *wu shu*. The monks who succeeded Bodhidharma did not cease their practice, and they perfected the art of combat. Tamo's lessons seemed to have borne fruit.

The art of the Shaolin monks was taught over the centuries in the shadows of the monastery's walls. Only monks were initiated into its practice, but a number of them left Shaolin to teach their art in other monasteries and even, sometimes, to lay people. Little by little the Shaolin pai became more popular, a trend that was only accentuated by the destruction of the monastery in 1723.

Chinese martial arts still bear a monastic imprint. The most widespread form of combat in China was and remains

Shaolin pai. But owing to the difficulty the majority of its practitioners had in understanding it, the art degenerated into a simple fighting method that relied more on muscular strength than the cultivation of inner quality.

Depressed by the decadence of this once noble art, some of its practitioners turned toward styles known as "internal," the arts of *nei chia*, which were perfected and transmitted within the close-knit circles of Taoist adepts.

## THE ART OF THE SOFT HAND

Legend declares that the person responsible for revitalizing *chuan shu*, the art of the fist, and for initiating the practice of the "internal" styles, was a Taoist ascetic with the mysterious name of Chang San Fong, the Master of the Three Peaks. Most certainly the heir to a thousand-year-old tradition, which he would then have taken up and adapted, this sage is generally presumed to be the man responsible for the birth of *wu tang shu*, "the art of the soft hand," generally assumed to have been the ancestor of tai chi chuan.

Translated as "the art of the supreme fist" or "ultimate boxing," tai chi chuan is often considered as no more than a simple therapeutic gymnastic routine of interest only to women and the elderly! Appearances can be deceiving; the movements are performed quite slowly, even after years of practice. More than one expert, however, has had cause to bitterly regret brushing up against a tai chi master the wrong way. The secret of this art resides in its name, the literal translation of which means the "action" *(chuan)* of the energy *(chi)* in the body *(tai)*. The true way of Taoist alchemy, tai chi chuan gives to the patient seeker the key to the science of energy. Hence a certain invulnerability may result—on the condition we don't forget that one of the names given to this art is "the struggle against one's shadow."

The second internal style is the *ba gua* that gets its name from the eight trigrams, the eight primordial elements according to the I Ching, the Book of Changes, which is the Taoist equivalent of the Bible. These eight trigrams are often represented in a circle that contains the harmonious symbol of yin (the passive forces) and yang (the active forces). The creator of *ba gua* was of course a Taoist ascetic. Quite close to tai chi, *ba gua* teaches the science of energy through continuous, circular movements. At the beginning of one's apprenticeship on this path, movements are made according to a very slow rhythm that is accelerated over the course of years of practice until it reaches a point of astounding rapidity, made possible by the long development of flexibility and fluidity.

*Hsing i* means "form, the action of the mind or spirit." This is the name of the third great internal art. The quest for harmony of the mind and body is the same as in the first two styles. Only the gestural work is different; it relies on a greater use of discontinuous linear movements that is more akin to Japanese karate.

Other styles of the art of the fist developed concurrently. Some degenerated rapidly into methods called "hard" or "external," in which strength predominates. Others are closer to the "internal" schools.

Certain evocatively named styles deserve mention: the "white heron" style; the "praying mantis" style; the "eagle's talons" style; the "radiant spring" style; the art of "the labyrinth"; the art of the "lost trail"; the art of the "eight tipsy deities"; and the art of the "drunken man." It is obvious that the Chinese found great inspiration in the study of nature. Some schools bear the name of an animal that serves the practitioners as a model. The majority of styles study every aspect of the attitudes and movements of a particular animal. The ideal model is of course the dragon, which combines the qualities of both tiger and snake: strength and flexibility, firmness and fluidity.

There is another point in common among all these schools. They all use the Tao, which like the Japanese *kata*, are movement sequences. They not only provide combat training but a symbolic gestural language and concentration exercises as well.

There are many different weapons used in the traditional Chinese martial arts: sword, saber, lance, staff, halberd, scythe, and so forth. Many schools that teach unarmed combat complete their teaching with courses in the use of weapons, which are considered to be extensions of the body and thus an excellent means of gaining mastery over it.

Though the unarmed hero remains the most popular in China, the Japanese have expressed a preference for the master of the sword, the samurai.

## BUDO AND THE BUJUTSU

Japanese martial arts are the heirs to the Chinese tradition in more than one respect. Japanese civilization, although strongly influenced by the Middle Kingdom, remains strikingly original in that the Land of the Rising Sun is a crucible that absorbs and integrates things to its own tastes.

The subtle sap of *budo* never ceased nurturing the martial arts in Japan. Fearful, perhaps, of contact with the West and the culture shock of the modern world, Japanese masters at the beginning of this century wished to emphasize the essential role played by the way *(do)* in their arts by changing the old names of the various *bujutsu* such as *jiujutsu, aiki-jutsu, ken-jutsu,* into judo, aikido, kendo, and so forth. Their hope was that the public at large would not confuse the martial arts with fighting sports, and the meaning of the way would not disappear into the byways of history.

The *bujutsu* are the two-directional conductors for *budo:* one allows it to reach us and the other allows us to reach it. Anyone who has attended a skilled demonstration or has had the chance to see Michel Random's magnificent film on this subject, has certainly seen the harmony of the movements and the beauty of the gestures. Numerous spectators have even compared these arts to virile dances or sacred ceremonies. This is a comparison that a boxing match or a football game certainly do not bring to mind!

Chance plays no role in this art. Technical research that has been underway since the dawn of time by Japanese masters capable of integrating the wisdom of their Chinese contemporaries has always been based on the complementary principles that govern the universe. The play between active (yang) and passive (yin) forces is put into practice with extraordinary precision in aggressive and defensive moves that are designed to neutralize an adversary with minimum effort and maximum efficiency. This has given rise to a stupefying gestural harmony, almost as if it were a naturally occurring phenomenon.

The *kata* are the primary embodiments of the breath of *budo*. The *kata* (forms, patterns) are sequences of predetermined movements. At first glance they seem to serve the purpose of allowing their practitioners to assimilate techniques and to teach their use for combat situations. But, when practiced correctly, there are also a number of beneficial effects attributed to them with regard to physical coordination, breath, rhythmic sense, concentration, and health. Masters used the *kata* to transmit their teachings, which included combat techniques and tactics, as well as spiritual symbolism. The *kata* are the bearers of a message that is coded on several levels, and they only give up their secrets after years or even a lifetime of intensive study. The origin of the *kata* is quite ancient, and the masters—both warriors and monks—who created them did so as a legacy for their students and for future generations in the hope that the form wouldn't be amputated from its heart and that the *bujutsu* would continue to serve the way.

## WEAPON BUJUTSU

Contrary to a widespread idea, Japanese martial arts were not the exclusive practice of the *bushi* class (better known as samurai). Commoners, especially monks, could become experienced practitioners and even masters.

We shouldn't confuse *bushido*, the way of the warrior, with *budo*, the way of the martial arts, though, because the use of the weapons of war was the privilege of the samurai, especially following the sixteenth century when a decree was enacted ordering the confiscation of all weapons then in the hands of the people.

Fencing, *ken-jutsu*, was the basic training of the samurai. The sword was the "bodyguard" of the warrior, who never let it out of his possession. Whether standing, seated, or lying down, a samurai had to be constantly ready to unsheathe his sword to save his life, which was ever at risk in feudal times. Once armed with the knowledge that an exhaustive display of swordsmanship was not necessary for vanquishing an adversary, the Japanese warrior began concentrating on perfecting to the highest degree his *iai:* the art of drawing his sword and striking his adversary before the latter even had a chance to adopt a defensive posture. As well as being the preeminent weapon of war, the sword also holds pride of place in numerous Japanese religious ceremonies. Furthermore, famous fencing schools were founded by Shinto priests such as those of the Kashima and Katori sanctuaries. Archery, *kyu-jutsu,* was another practice that along with *ken-jutsu* was reserved for the aristocracy. With the appearance of firearms the bow began to disappear from the battlefields, but *kyu-jutsu* gained in purity, becoming a discipline centered on spiritual development because the archer in the *dojo* has only himself to fight in order to hit the target. Archery has survived principally in the temples, where it still remains a daily ritual for many monks. The Japanese consider *kyu-jutsu* to be one of the greatest religious symbols because "With one end of his bow the archer pierces heaven, with the other, he penetrates the earth. Stretched between the two, the bowstring hurls the arrow into the heart of both the visible and the invisible target."

*Naginata-jutsu* is the technique of fighting with scythes. The warrior monks known as the *yama bushi* were the first to make use of this weapon in Japan. These renowned *yama bushi* (meaning "mountain warriors") were Buddhist monks who lived on the slopes of Mount Hiei. They were organized into military orders, much like the Knights Templar in the West, to assure the safety of temple sanctuaries against bandits. The *yama bushi* were formidable combatants whose monasteries quickly became important centers of the martial arts and whose reputation was known throughout Japan. Countless samurai went there for instruction and to perfect their skills. With regard to *naginata-jutsu*, we should mention that the *yama bushi* were particularly skilled in the use of war scythes. The famous monk Benkei, the companion of the most popular hero of Japanese history, Yoshishutne, entered into legend with a *naginata* in his hand. Another twelfth-century monk, Tajima "the Arrow Cutter," safely crossed a bridge swept by volleys of arrows that he calmly mowed down with his *naginata!* The use of this weapon soon spread to every rank of samurai. With the introduction of firearms the use of the *naginata* also declined, but it remained the weapon of choice in aristocratic homes where it was used by samurai wives to defend their hearths. *Naginata-jutsu* is still the principal feminine martial art in Japan.

In the sixteenth century, weapons of war were officially forbidden to the people, including even monks, in order to safeguard the dominant social position of the aristocratic class of the *bushi*.

Peasants and artisans transformed their tools into astonishing weapons. The flails used to beat rice became nunchakus, sickles became *kama*, and so forth, and all soon became worthy rivals to the sword. *Bo-jutsu* was without doubt the martial art practiced most by the majority of the Japanese people because the *bo*, the staff, is a simple instrument of everyday use. But in the hands of a master it can be the most effective of weapons. Vagabonds, pilgrims, monks, and wandering artists often owed their survival on the brigand-haunted roads of medieval Japan to their skill with the staff. The renowned Zen poet Basho (1643–94), one of the greatest of all Japanese poets, had a reputation for handling the *bo* stick with as much flair as he did language. The value of these popular combat arts was eventually realized by the samurai, who practiced them rigorously after learning of their battle worthiness firsthand, and often at their own expense, if only to better defend themselves against them.

In any event, most masters attained their highest levels only after they had assimilated several martial arts practices, which allowed them to extract the common principles that bound them together and to understand better the essence of the way.

All the *bujutsu* just mentioned depend upon an artificial instrument: they can be used or studied only if the practitioner carries a weapon. In addition to weapon *bujutsu*, the arts of barehanded combat were also widespread.

## BAREHAND BUJUTSU

When a man is disarmed during combat, his last and best chance of survival rests in his ability to make use of his natural weapons, those his own body provides.

*Jiujutsu*, or the art of flexibility, is a method of barehanded combat that is based on the principle of nonresistance. This art primarily uses techniques that allow one to take advantage of an adversary's moves in order to neutralize him. *Jiujutsu* is a complete method in itself that makes use of the entire arsenal of the body: dodges, strikes, sweeping movements, punches, grabs, and strangleholds. The sport judo, which derives from *jiujutsu* but has grown quite far from the art refined by Jigoro Kano at the beginning of this century, is only a shadowy reflection that has been impoverished and mutilated.

*Aiki-jutsu* means the art of the harmonization of energies. Quite close to *jiujutsu* in its techniques, this martial art never gained the same popularity as the others because it was taught secretly within certain families of the martial nobility. The Takeda family was one of the keepers of this tradition, and it was only at the beginning of the twentieth century that the last surviving member of the Takeda lineage, Sokaku, consented to divulge a small part of this teaching. Ueshiba Morihei was accepted as one of his students and his creation of aikido was largely inspired by his understanding of this art. Aikido is a martial art based on nonviolence and stripped of any offensive techniques.

Barehanded combat arts of Chinese origin were also widespread in Japan; these are the *kempo*. Karate is the best known of these *kempo*. In Japanese, *karate* means "empty hand."

The island of Okinawa in the Ryukyu archipelago, south of Japan, fell under Chinese control in the fifteenth century. The occupiers forbade the possession of arms by the natives. Far from resigning themselves to their fate, the people of

Okinawa clandestinely developed a martial art derived from the Chinese *kempo:* the *toda* or "hand of China." This art was primarily introduced by Chinese monks, as is still shown by the names of certain *kata:* one *kata* comes from Jion-ji, an ancient Buddhist temple; the Shorin-ryu style explicitly evokes its affiliation with the Shaolin temple. The prohibition was maintained when the island was taken over by a Japanese lord in 1609. Practiced all the more—always in secret and always at night—the local martial art began to make a name for itself as Okinawate. It was not until the twentieth century that Funakoshi Gishin introduced it into the rest of Japan. He decided at that time to call this art *karate-do,* "the way of the empty hand," in order to emphasize its affiliation with the *budo.* The word *kara* ("empty") was chosen not only to designate the barehanded nature of this martial art, but also, primarily, to stress its moral and religious significance; *kara* also refers to the "lack of all aggressive intention" and evokes the Zen experience of "emptiness."

This appears to be quite far from the violent reputation that karate currently enjoys. Its techniques are, in fact, quite formidable because they specialize in *atemi:* blows directed against vital body points with the aid of the hands, feet, elbows, and knees. If it is not practiced in its traditional guise as an art of defense and a school of the way, karate, detached from the *do,* can easily degenerate into a dangerous form of boxing that has lost any kinship to the *karate-do* practiced by Funakoshi Gishin until his death at age eighty-nine.

# 2

## On the Threshold of the Mystery

*When an old man moves an enormous weight*
*or successfully resists the attack of several*
*young men, it obviously doesn't have*
*anything to do with strength, and how*
*would speed be a factor, either?*

### WANG CHUNG YUEH

The life story of Master Ueshiba Morihei, the founder of aikido, is full of extraordinary events. During his life he was attacked completely unexpectedly on more than one occasion, from behind as well as when he was sleeping. He was never caught off guard, however, and he always successfully neutralized his opponents. One day he accepted a challenge to fight unarmed a kendo expert armed with a *boken* (a wooden sword). He dodged every blow until his exhausted adversary stopped his attack. Master Ueshiba explained: "Before someone attacks me his *ki* comes toward me. If I evade it, and his body follows his *ki*, I have only to touch him lightly to make him fall to the ground."

During an expedition in Mongolia, he did something even

more astounding. A soldier had him in the sights of his rifle and at a distance of about six yards. At the very moment he fired, the soldier had the unpleasant surprise of being assaulted by Ueshiba, who succeeded in disarming him. The master reportedly said in reference to this incident: "There is a long moment of time between the moment when a man decides to fire and his actually firing." Did Ueshiba have the ability to play with time? Was he capable of escaping the laws of physics?

It is certain that a man such as Ueshiba is an enigma who becomes quite an embarrassment to Cartesian and official science, all the more so since these feats cannot simply be written off as more examples of the superstitious credulity of the medieval period. Ueshiba Morihei was a contemporary master who died in 1969. Numerous witnesses, still alive, can provide testimony for what they saw with their own eyes. There are even photographs in which Ueshiba, a frail old man of eighty years, can be seen with his body relaxed and a smile on his lips, resisting the vigorous shoves and pushes of a much younger man.

These strange powers are common to all the martial arts. They constitute the science of *chi* in Chinese and *ki* in Japanese, an admittedly difficult notion to translate into English. *Ki* simultaneously signifies breath, inner energy, attention, spirit, and mind. To complicate matters, different qualities of *ki* exist. According to Eastern tradition, the original *ki* is still spreading throughout the entire universe and is gradually deteriorating as it draws further away from its source, the Tao. It thus imbues the beings and things of the cosmos in varying degrees of intensity, according to their level.

Techniques of breath, concentration, and meditation are taught with the objective of learning to feel and to master *ki*.

The *kiai*, vulgarly called the "shout that kills," is in fact the art of directing and projecting *ki*. Two aspects of *kiai* exist: a loud cry that produces a certain vibrational quality and comes from the *hara tanden*, the vital center located in the lower belly. *Hara* is the center of gravity in the body that is responsible for stability and movement. Any movement will attain its maximum effectiveness if it has been initiated by the *hara;* it will be blocked if it results only from a muscular contraction. The second aspect of *kiai* is the phenomenon known as the "silent shout," which arises from the very depths of the individual. This shout projects a subtle energy that can sometimes be produced by the eyes, so it is really quite similar to hypnosis. The goal of the shouts—both sounded and silent—is the same: to create vibrations capable of alarming one's adversary, but they can also serve to reanimate someone who has lost consciousness as a result of the shock caused by these vibrations.

*Kime* is the act of projecting *ki* with the help of the body, but gathering the shock wave and internal energy together in one point in a way that will allow this energy to persist after the strike. Karate masters sometimes perform a strange experiment: a student holds a pad folded in half and then in half again against his abdomen, not forgetting to clench his abdominal muscles. The master will then give the pad a relaxed kick while projecting *kime*. Everytime the student will drop the mattress to clutch his belly, unable to stop himself from uttering a cry of pain. The energy has traveled through the mattress and contracted abdominal muscles to strike the student's spinal column!

The sixth sense, the ability to foresee an attack, also has a relation to *ki* energy. Every thought and intention is a wave put out by an individual that can be caught and harnessed by someone with greatly developed sensitivity. All the great masters possess this power of intuitively sensing an attack, something that comes from years of practice. This gives them the ability to predict every move an adversary makes and evade any attack, despite their advanced age.

In itself, *ki* is neither good nor bad. The *kiai* can be used to "paralyze" or restore consciousness. The person using the *ki* is the one who makes it evil or beneficial, destructive or creative. The use of various powers can be debased and corrupted to serve the evil ends of an egotistic individual. The wisdom schools worthy of the name were therefore quite strict in selecting their students, and the transmission of such techniques occurred only under the seal of secrecy.

In any case, the mastery of powers is not the true goal of the way. This mastery is simply a consequence of the awakening of latent faculties that exist in every human being and that result from certain kinds of inner work necessary for self-realization. The masters rarely made use of their power, either in self-defense or in teaching demonstrations. Utilization of these powers and energy manipulation was never done gratuitously. The fear of a backlash was always justified. This is the law of karma: one reaps as one sows. Someone who abuses these powers wastes his energy and buries himself in a dark labyrinth, thus losing any chance of gaining true mastery or gaining access to the ultimate secret.

Through a door pushed ajar to an unknown world, these narratives of "extraordinary powers" give us a sense of an impalpable reality.

Is the science of energy totally beyond our grasp? Are not the universe and humanity both fantastic enigmas?

## The Invisible Target

While Master Kenzo Awa was explaining that the art of archery consisted in letting the arrow fly with no intention of success, in other words, to fire without aiming, his European student Herrigel couldn't stop himself from asking, "If that is true, shouldn't you be able to shoot blindfolded?"

The master stood and gazed at his student thoughtfully for a long moment . . . then set a date for him to come by that very evening.

It was already night when Herrigel was let into the *dojo*. Master Awa first invited him to partake in *cha no yu*, the tea ceremony, which he performed himself. Without saying a word, the old man carefully prepared the tea then served it with an infinite delicacy. Each of his gestures was made with a precision and beauty that only the greatest concentration can provide. Both men guarded their silence in order to savor all the nuances of this harmonious ritual. As the Japanese say, it was a moment of eternity.

Followed by his visitor, the master then crossed the *dojo* until he was facing the hall that housed the targets, sixty yards further away. The target hall was unlit and even its outlines were hard to make out. Following the master's instructions, Herrigel went in and set up a target without turning on the light.

When he was done and had come back, he saw that the old archer was standing in readiness for the ceremony of shooting the bow. After bowing in the direction of the invisible target, the master shifted his position as if he were gliding across the floor. His movements flowed with the slowness and fluidity of a puff of smoke spiraling gently in the wind. He lifted his arms then lowered them. He held the bow serenely in his hands until he abruptly shot the arrow. It disappeared into the gloom. The master remained motionless, his arms suspended, as if he were accompanying the arrow toward its unknown destination, as if the actual act of firing the bow was still continuing on another plane. Then the bow and arrow danced in his hands again. The second arrow whistled off, in turn to be swallowed by the night.

Herrigel hurried to illuminate the hall, impatient to see where the arrows had landed. The first was in the very heart of the target. The second was just next to it, slightly pushed from its flight path by the presence of the first arrow, which had been pushed aside, bursting several centimeters of its bamboo butt.

When carrying back the target, Herrigel congratulated the master for his feat. But the latter responded, "I deserve no credit. This happened because I allowed 'something' to happen in me. It is this 'something' that allowed the arrows to use the bow in order to join with the target."

This stupefying exploit is recounted by Professor Herrigel in his book *Zen in the Art of Archery,* in which he relates the events of his taxing apprenticeship during the six years he spent studying *kyudo* in Japan.

### The Sixth Sense

Tajima no Kami, the shogun's fencing instructor, was walking in his garden on a beautiful spring afternoon. He appeared to be completely absorbed in the contemplation of his flowering cherry trees. A young servant followed several feet behind him, carrying his sword. An idea flashed through the young man's mind: "Despite all my master's skill with the sword, it would be easy to attack him from behind right now, since he is so engrossed in the charms of the cherry-tree flowers." At that very instant, Tajima no Kami turned back and looked around, as if he were seeking for someone in hiding. Disturbed, he started poking through all the nooks and crannies of the garden. Not finding anyone, he retired to his room, in a pensive frame of mind. One of his servants eventually asked him if he felt all right and if there were anything anyone could do for him. Tajima answered, "I am deeply disturbed by a strange incident for which I can find no explanation. Thanks to my long practice of the martial arts, I can sense any aggressive thought directed against me. While I was in the garden, that is precisely what I felt. Other than my servant, no one was there, not even a dog. Not having found any justification for my perception, I am very disappointed in myself."

When the young man learned of this, he approached his master and admitted the idea he had briefly entertained while walking behind him. He humbly craved his master's forgiveness. Tajima no Kami relaxed and went back out into his garden with his mind at ease.

## Bokuden and His Three Sons

One day the great sword master Bokuden received a visit from one of his colleagues. As a means of introducing his three sons to his friend and to demonstrate the level they had attained following his teachings, Bokuden devised a little stratagem: he propped a vase on a sliding door in such a way that it would fall on the head of anyone entering the room.

Calmly sitting with his friend facing the door, Bokuden called for his eldest son. When the latter arrived he suddenly stopped short in front of the door. After pushing it half open, he took down the vase before entering. Closing the door behind him, he replaced the vase before bowing to the two masters. "This is my eldest son," said Bokuden with a smile, "he has already achieved a high level and is well on his way to becoming a master."

The second son was called. He slid the door open and started to enter the room. Barely dodging the vase that was heading for his skull, he managed to catch it in midair. "This is my second son," Bokuden explained to his guest, "he still has a long way to go."

When the youngest son's turn came, he rushed into the room and took the vase fully on the neck. But before the vase could fall to the tatami, he drew his sword and cut it in half. "And this," resumed the master, "is my youngest son. He's the black sheep of the family, but he's still young."

## The Warrior's Eye

A fervent fan of No theater, Tajima no Kami was attending a performance at which the entire court was present. The greatest actor of the time was performing. Tajima attentively watched his performance, which revealed a great self-mastery. His concentration appeared flawless and his gestures left no openings, just like a veteran soldier. Not having taken his eyes off the actor for a single second since the beginning of the performance, Master Kajima pushed a shout of *kiai* toward the actor. It was a discreet shout, but it didn't go unnoticed.

A murmur went through the audience. Looks were exchanged. The shogun himself turned around to see what was the matter.

Once the performance was concluded, the shogun hastened to summon Tajima no Kami to ask the reason for his strange behavior. The master contented himself with saying, "Ask the actor, he knows why."

In fact the actor admitted that, "the *kiai* echoed at the very moment I experienced a momentary distraction because something in the decor had changed."

### Infallible Concentration

Sen no Rikyu remains one of the most illustrious masters of *cha no yu,* the tea ceremony, in Japanese memory. He was in the service of Hideyoshi, the *kampaku* who governed the land at that time.

One day, while Master Rikyu was officiating at a tea ceremony, Hideyoshi remarked to his generals, "Pay attention to how Rikyu prepares the tea and you will notice that his body is filled with *ki*, that his gestures are measured and precise like those of a great warrior. He offers not a single opening. His concentration is flawless."

To the mind of the famous general Kato Kiyomasa came the idea of verifying whether what the *kampaku* was saying was as exact as he would have them believe. He decided to try and touch the officiant with his fan once an opening presented itself. Absorbed in this game, he began attentively watching Sen no Rikyu, who was right next to him. After several minutes, believing he spotted a flaw in Rikyu's performance, the general started to point his fan. At that precise instant, the tea master looked him straight in the eyes and smiled.

Kiyomasa felt his breath cut short. His fan fell from his hands.

## The Incredible Power of Chi

There was once a master of barehanded combat who taught his art in a provincial village. His reputation in the region was such that he defied all competition; the students would have nothing to do with any of the other teachers. A young expert who had been attempting to establish himself as a teacher in the area decided one day to seek a fight with the famous master and put an end to his reign.

The expert presented himself at the master's school, where an old man met him at the door to ask what he wanted. With no hesitation the young man proclaimed his intention. The old man, visibly embarrassed, tried to explain to him how suicidal that idea was, given the master's formidable abilities.

To impress this driveling old fool who seemed to entertain doubts about his strength, the expert took hold of a board that was leaning in a corner and, with a single strike of his knee, broke it in two. The old man remained calm and composed. The visitor repeated his demand for a match with the master, threatening to break everything in the place as evidence of his determination and abilities. The old man than begged him to wait a moment and left the room.

He returned shortly, holding an enormous piece of bamboo in his hand. He gave it to the young man saying, "The master customarily breaks pieces of bamboo of this size with a single strike of his fist. I cannot take your request seriously if you aren't capable of doing this as well."

The presumptuous young claimant tried to subject the bamboo to the same fate as the board, but finally had to give up; he was exhausted and all his limbs were aching. He declared that no man could break such a piece of bamboo with his bare hands. The old man answered that there was one man who could: the master. He advised his visitor to abandon his scheme as long as he was incapable of performing this feat. Overcome, the expert swore to return one day and successfully pass this test.

Two years passed during which time the expert trained himself intensively with the aim of breaking that bamboo.

Each day he got a little stronger and his body became a little tougher. His efforts eventually bore fruit, and he once again showed up at the door to the school, brimming with self-confidence.

Demanding that someone bring him one of the famous bamboo pieces for the test, the visitor didn't delay propping it up between two stones. He concentrated several seconds, raised his hand, then broke the bamboo while uttering a terrible shout. With a satisfied smile on his lips he turned back to the frail old man. The old man made a little face and stated, "Definitely, what I've done is unforgivable. I believe I forgot to mention one little detail: the master breaks the bamboo without touching it." Beside himself, the young man replied that he didn't believe in the deeds of the master whose existence he hadn't even been able to verify.

Then grabbing a solid piece of bamboo, the old man hung it by a string from the ceiling. After taking several deep breaths, during which time his eyes didn't quit the bamboo even for an instant, he emitted a terrifying shout that came from the very depths of his being, and his hand cleft the air like a sword, only to come to a complete stop several inches from the bamboo—which shattered.

Subdued by the shock of what he had just seen, the expert remained motionless for several minutes, petrified and incapable of saying a word. Finally he humbly craved the old master's pardon for his odious behavior and begged to be accepted as a student.

## The Secret of Proficiency

Although an expert and renowned teacher of the art of swordsmanship, Ito Ittosai was far from satisfied with the level of his knowledge. Despite his efforts, he was fully aware that he had not managed to make any progress for some period of time.

In despair he decided to follow the example of the Buddha. The sutras recounted how the latter had sat beneath a fig tree to meditate, firmly resolved not to budge until he had received the ultimate understanding of existence and the universe. Determined to die on the spot rather than renounce his intention, the Buddha achieved his vow and awoke to the Supreme Truth. Ito Ittosai therefore made his way to a temple in order to discover the secret of the art of the sword. He devoted seven days and seven nights to his meditation.

On the dawn of the eighth day, worn out and discouraged by his failure to learn anything more, he resigned himself to returning home and abandoning all hope of piercing the famous secret.

After leaving the temple his path led through a wooded lane. He had hardly taken a few steps when he suddenly felt a threatening presence behind him. Without taking the time to think, he turned around while simultaneously drawing his weapon.

It was then that he saw how his spontaneous gesture had saved his life: a bandit lay at his feet, sword in hand.

## The Magic Coat

Yang Lu Chan, following a visit that had lasted late into the night, was returning home. As he was crossing through one of the most disreputable quarters of Peking, he walked with great strides, hoping to avoid any irritating encounters.

But just then a disagreeable surprise awaited him: on the next street corner he found himself face to face with a gang of young thugs who barred his passage. Turning around to flee the other way, he bitterly observed that his retreat was cut off by the rest of the gang. Around thirty ruffians, armed with sticks and truncheons, surrounded him. Yang Lu Chan didn't even try to resist; he let them strip him of his purse without saying a word and, when their blows began raining down on him, curled up in his coat and allowed himself to fall to the ground. The thugs unleashed a storm of kicks and blows with their clubs on Yang who, wrapped in his coat, resembled a punching bag. His aggressors quickly grew weary of punching this inanimate body and thinking he was done for, fled and left him lying there in the street.

The next day, Yang Lu Chan, strolled through town and performed his normal daily activities as if nothing had happened. In any case, he bore not a single trace of the blows he had suffered the previous night. But the most surprising thing about this story is the fact that several of his attackers were confined to their beds! Those who had made direct physical contact with Yang's coat woke to find their limbs paralyzed for several days.

Yang Lu Chan (1799–1872) was, in fact, the most famous tai chi chuan master of his day. Although challenged on countless occasions, he was never defeated. So it seems that in the matter of this nocturnal ambush, in order not to risk killing one of his assailants, Yang chose to deaden their blows with his "magic coat."

In China it is said that certain masters have attained a level in which their *chi*, their internal energy, is so powerful that it has made their bodies invulnerable, as supple as cotton, and ungraspable. But, on the other hand, when they touch someone, that person feels the master's true strength, similar to that of a mountain, and is paralyzed by it as if he had received an electrical shock from a high-tension wire.

## Like Sword Maker, Like Sword

"The sword is the soul of the samurai," we are told by one of the oldest maxims of the *bushido*, the way of the warrior. A symbol of virility, loyalty, and courage, the sword was the preferred weapon of the samurai. But in Japanese tradition the sword is more than an awesome instrument of war, and more than a mere philosophical symbol: it is a magic weapon. It can be malevolent or benevolent according to the personality of its maker and its owner. The sword is like an extension of the person handling it. It is mysteriously imbued with the vibrations that emanate from his being.

The ancient Japanese, inspired by the Shinto religion, could only conceive of the fabrication of a sword as an alchemical work in which the inner harmony of the smith is more important than his technical abilities. Before forging a blade, the master blacksmith would spend several days meditating. Then after cleansing himself with ablutions of cold water and dressing himself in white, he would set to work with the best inner conditions for creating a quality weapon.

Masamune and Murasama were skilled smiths who lived at the beginning of the sixteenth century. Both of them manufactured swords of exceedingly great quality. Murasama had a violent character and was a disturbing and taciturn figure. He had the sinister reputation of forging dreadful blades that provoked their owners into bloody combats and sometimes even wounded those who used them. These bloodthirsty weapons quickly acquired a reputation as malefic instruments. In contrast, Masamune was a smith of great serenity who performed purification rituals before forging his blades. Today, they are considered the very best in Japan.

A man who wished to test the difference in quality between the two methods of creating a sword placed one of

Murasama's swords in a stream. Each leaf floating on the surface that came into contact with the blade was cut in two. Then he placed a sword manufactured by Masamune in the water. The leaves seemed to avoid the blade. Not a single one was cut; all floated past the entire length of the sharpened side of the blade and remained whole, as if the sword wished to spare them.

This man then pronounced his judgment, "The Murasama is terrible, the Masamune is humane."

# 3

# Confronting the Mountain

*As long as you are incapable of*
*going beyond the mountain, it is*
*impossible to attain the Way.*

## WEI KUAN

Tradition tells us that following the way is akin to scaling a steep mountain. The person who has chosen to undertake that ascent will select the slope he wishes to attempt and set off in search of a guide who can show him the path. These choices are deciding factors. If the slope is too steep, or the guide too inexperienced, the results can be disastrous. But nothing is guaranteed, even with the best possible guide. There are numerous obstacles ahead and many painful efforts will have to be undertaken. A great struggle that involves going one-on-one with the mountain is necessary. One's muscles are straining, one's fingers are tightly clinging to the rock. Each movement must be precise and measured. Nothing can be left to chance. One false step will lead to a long fall.

But what is the point of this challenge that does not let up for a second, poised halfway between the summit and the abyss, between life and death?

The person who dares the mountain knows, or at least something within him or her knows, that the great struggle takes place inside. The mountain is only a pretext. It permits a man or woman to come face-to-face with him- or herself, it provides one with an opportunity to go beyond oneself. It is by coming to grips with these kinds of difficulties that the student will develop the discipline, the will, and the energy necessary to his continued evolution. In reality every ordeal is a help in getting to the way. "If Heaven is about to entrust an important mission to a man, it begins by filling his heart with bitterness and by confusing his powers of perception and overturning his plans. It forces him to exert his bone and muscle. It forces him to endure hunger and all manner of sufferings. When the man emerges triumphantly over all these trials and tribulations, he is then capable of accomplishing what would have been impossible for him to do before." This quote from Mencius is a very precise answer to the question: "What is the true meaning of life?"

What is truly at stake in this inner battle? For the masters, the real obstacles that prevent the student from making any progress are those erected by his or her artificial personality. The ordinary individual, choking under a yoke of mental and physical habits, his vision of the world distorted by a screen of illusions, is an invalid cut off from the depths of his being, depths whose potential remains untouched. The necessary work to be done consists in exploding these physical and psychological blocks so that the individual's latent forces can blossom freely. The goal of *budo,* the way of combat, like any authentic path, is the regeneration of the individual. But this self-realization can only be attained through a merciless struggle against one's own defects, weaknesses, and illusions. Vanquishing one's inner obstacles requires the patience to be relentless in tracking them down and the courage to confront them when that search bears fruit. Pride, cowardice, impatience, and doubt, all fed by illusion, are so many dreadful traps in which a great many people have fallen. The path through them twists like a snake; it is long, difficult, and taxing. Not allowing oneself to become discouraged, persevering no matter what and in spite of oneself, is one of the keys to the way.

It should not be forgotten, as stated by D. T. Suzuki, that "as long as one will not eat the bread of sorrow, one cannot know the flavor of real life."

### Not So Stupid

Yagyu Tajima no Kami had an ape for his animal familiar. This animal frequently attended the classes he gave his students. Being by nature a great copycat, the ape learned how to hold and use a sword. He became an expert—for a member of his species.

One day, a *ronin* (a masterless samurai) expressed his desire to have a friendly spear match with Tajima no Kami.

The master suggested he first engage in a match with the ape. The visitor felt as if he had been rudely insulted, but agreed to the match nonetheless.

Armed with his spear, the *ronin* made a swift assault on the ape, who was wielding a *shinai* (a bamboo sword). The animal adroitly evaded the thrusts of the spear. Counterattacking, the animal managed to get near his adversary and strike him. The *ronin* then retreated and set his weapon in a defensive position. Taking advantage of this, the ape leaped on the spear handle and disarmed the warrior. When the *ronin*, in complete misery, returned to Tajima no Kami, the master made the following remark: "I knew from the beginning that you weren't capable of beating the ape."

From that day the *ronin* ceased his visits to the master. Several months had gone by when he suddenly reappeared. He expressed his desire to have another bout with the ape. The master, observing that the *ronin* had undergone extensive training since they had last seen each other, had a feeling that the ape would refuse to fight. Thus he did not agree to his visitor's request. The *ronin* continued to insist, and finally the Master ceded to his visitor's wishes.

The moment the ape caught sight of the man he was to fight, he threw down his weapon and fled screaming.

Tajima no Kami said in conclusion, "Didn't I tell you this would happen."

Shortly thereafter, he recommended the *ronin* to the service of one of his friends.

## An Accelerated Teaching

A famous sword master's son, Matajuro Yagyu, was renounced by his father, who felt that his son's work was too mediocre for there to be any hope of him becoming a master.

Matajuro, who had determined, despite everything, to become a master swordsman, left for Mount Futara to meet the famous master Banzo. But Banzo only confirmed his father's judgment. "You will never be able to meet the necessary conditions."

"But if I work extremely hard, how many years will it take me to become a master?" the young man persisted.

"The rest of your life," answered Banzo.

"I can't wait that long. I am ready to endure anything so long as I can follow your teaching. If I become your devoted servitor, how much time will it take?"

"Oh, maybe ten years."

"But, you know, my father is getting old and I will soon have to take care of him. If I practice even more intensively, how many years will it take?"

"Oh, maybe thirty."

"But, how can that be?! First ten, now thirty. Believe me, I am ready to undergo anything in order to master this art in the shortest time possible!"

"Oh well, in that case you will have to remain with me for seventy years. A man in as much of a hurry as you are to obtain results can hardly learn anything quickly," explained Banzo.

"Very well," declared Matajuro, finally comprehending that his impatience was to blame, "I will be your servitor."

Matajuro was then told he was no longer allowed to talk about fencing or even touch a sword. He served the master, making his meals, cleaning his house, and taking care of the garden, all without a word on the subject of swords. He was not even permitted to watch the other students training.

Three years passed. Matajuro worked constantly and often brooded over his sorry fate that had stolen away any possibility of studying the art to which he had planned to devote his life. Then one day, while cleaning and ruminating about his sorrows, Banzo snuck up behind him and gave him a terrible blow with a *boken* (wooden sword). On the next day, while Matajuro was preparing rice, the master again attacked him completely unexpectedly. From then on, Matajuro had to defend himself night and day from Banzo's surprise attacks.

He had to remain on his guard every instant of the day, in total awareness, so as not to be struck by his master's sword. He learned so rapidly that his concentration, speed, and a kind of sixth sense that he developed, soon allowed him to avoid Banzo's attacks. One day, perhaps less than ten years after his arrival, the master told him there was nothing else he could teach him.

## The Thief of Knowledge

Born in a Ho Pei peasant family at the beginning of the nineteenth century, the young Yang Lu Chan had but one passion: *chuan shu,* the art of the fist. Having diligently frequented the martial arts schools of his province from childhood, he had become a reputed expert in very little time. But the styles he had practiced up to that time were not satisfying. He was aware of the fact that, since the destruction of the Shaolin monastery, the art of the fist had degenerated into a combat method that gave too great a place to recipes for techniques and muscular strength. Despite his search through every nook and cranny in Ho Pei, he had not managed to discover even one master capable of teaching him a more profound form of the art that would lead to the way of harmony.

His growing despair came to an end when he heard talk of tai chi chuan, an art that was gaining popularity in Hunan province.

Leaving his friends and relatives behind, Yang undertook a 400-mile journey on foot in order to reach the land of the art he wished to study. As soon as he could, he found admission into the hermetic world of tai chi adepts. In the course of his conversations with these practitioners, one name was mentioned constantly, that of Master Chen Chang Hsiang. This man was generally regarded at that time as having the greatest "kung fu," in other words, the greatest experience. But, unfortunately, Master Chen taught only the members of his family, and in conditions of the greatest secrecy.

Yang thought to himself that the long journey he had taken deserved to be rewarded by study with the best possible teacher. He skillfully managed to secure a position in the Chen family as a servant. Every day, he managed to find a way to spy on the training sessions provided by the family patriarch. Carefully hidden, he attentively observed the movements and drank in the master's words and counsel. During the night when everyone else was asleep, he zealously reperformed what he had seen that day and tirelessly worked on polishing his grasp of the sequences he had seen on days previous.

His spying lasted several months without raising any suspicions, right up to the day he was caught red-handed. Immediately led before Master Chen, he expected the worst. The old man indeed appeared quite upset and the tone of his voice betrayed a certain amount of irritation:

"Well, young man, it would appear that you have abused our trust in you. You found yourself a position here with the sole aim of spying on our teaching, am I right?"

"That is so," Yang admitted.

"I still don't know what we are going to do with you. While we are deciding, I am curious to see what you were able to learn under such conditions. Could you give me a demonstration?"

Yang then executed an exercise sequence with such concentration and fluidity of movement that the old Chen was deeply moved to see such a faithful reflection of his art. He kept a tight grip on his emotions and remained silent for a long moment before saying:

"It would be stupid to let you leave with the little you know. You would risk staining the reputation of our family by demonstrating our art incompletely. The best solution is for you to remain here long enough to finish your apprenticeship, and this time, under my supervision!"

Remaining for many more years with the Chen family, Yang integrated in an increasingly profound manner the supreme art of tai chi. It was not until he had received his old master's blessing that he returned to his native province.

In Peking, where he decided to settle and teach his art, it wasn't long until he was called the "unsurpassable Yang." Indeed, although often challenged by other teachers or young champions, he was never defeated. His bouts with challengers contributed even more to the reinforcement of tai chi chuan's reputation by virtue of the fact that he always succeeded in neutralizing his opponents without wounding them.

## The Master of the Three Peaks

Chang San Fong, the Master of the Three Peaks, was tall in stature, slim in build, and robust in constitution, all contributing to his formidable appearance. His face, which was round here and square there, was adorned with a spiky beard that looked like a forest of halberds. A thick bun was enthroned on the top of his skull. Although his appearance was fierce, his gaze expressed tender tranquility and benevolence.

He always wore the same tunic made out of a single piece of braided bamboo—in summer and winter, alike—and the most common object seen in his hand was a fly swatter made from a horse tail.

Thirsty for knowledge, he spent the greater part of his life making pilgrimages to the slopes of Mount Sichuan, Mount Chansi, and Mount Ho Pei. He visited the most important Taoist sites, going from one monastery to another, staying in sanctuaries and temples that the steep slopes of the mountains made difficult to reach. He was quickly initiated into the practice of meditation by the Taoist masters. Everywhere he went he studied the sacred books and ceaselessly sought the answers to the mysteries of the universe.

One day, after he had been silently meditating for some hours, he heard a marvelous, supernatural song. Looking around, he saw a bird on the branch of a tree staring fixedly at the ground. At the foot of the tree a snake was rearing its head to the sky. The eyes of the bird and the snake met, their glances confronted one another. Suddenly, giving vent to piercing cries, the bird dove on the snake and tried to attack it with furious blows from his claws and beak. The snake, undulating in a fluid movement, skillfully dodged the violent attacks of his assailant. The bird, exhausted by his fruitless efforts, returned to the branch he had been sitting on to regain his strength. Then he resumed his assault. The snake continued his circular dance that little by little transformed into a spiral of swirling, unseizeable energy.

Legend tells us that Chang San Fong was inspired by this sight to create the wu tang pai, the style of the "flexible hand," which, fashioned by generations of Taoists, became the tai chi chuan we know today.

This is why the movements of tai chi have no beginning or end. They unfurl pliantly like the silken thread of a cocoon, and they flow without interruption like the waters of the Yangtze River.

### The Image of Asari

At the age of twenty-seven, Yamaoka Tesshu, who had already made a name for himself as an expert swordsman, fought with Asari Matashichiro, who was also a famous sword fighter. This match was brief because Asari quickly disarmed his young adversary.

Shaken to his depths, Yamaoka experienced unending distress not because of his defeat, but because he realized how much he lacked spiritual maturity. Motivated by this encounter he redoubled his efforts to devote himself entirely to training in *ken-jutsu* (the art of the sword) and seated meditation *(zazen)*.

Desiring to put to the test the level he had attained after ten years of intensive practice, he arranged a second meeting with Asari. In the course of this second bout, he felt how his adversary dominated him and, paralyzed by the air of mastery Asari gave off, broke off the fight and acknowledged his defeat.

This latest match made such an impression upon him that he was now haunted by the image of Asari, an obsessive image that ceaselessly reminded him of his mediocrity. Far from resigning himself, he intensified his practice with both sword and meditation. Seven years passed when, following a profound spiritual experience, he suddenly realized that Asari's image had ceased tormenting him. He then decided to measure himself against his former adversary once more.

Asari first engaged in a match with one of his students but the student admitted his defeat before the fight had barely begun. Yamaoka then met Asari for the third time. The two men faced each other for a long moment, appraising each other with their eyes. Suddenly, Asari lowered his sword and declared, "You are there, you are finally on the way."

# 4

## The Snare of Appearances

*When the eagle attacks, he dives without*
*extending his wings. When the tiger is about*
*to leap on his prey, he crawls with his ears*
*laid back. By the same token, when a sage is*
*on the point of acting, no one can sense it.*

### FUNAKOSHI GISHIN

"Underestimating one's adversary is like losing one's treasure," is an ancient Chinese proverb. The person who plays his adversary's game has indeed already lost.

Numerous experts have achieved a certain renown thanks to feints and secret weapons they can handle with skill. There is a vast arsenal of ruses, tactics, and "assorted tricks" of all kinds. The adversary can retreat, the better to launch a counterattack, seem to hesitate, the better to surprise, and appear weak and inexperienced when in truth he is a formidable fighter. A famous school of *chuan shu* (the drunkard's style) founded its entire methodology on just this concept. Its disciples study and train themselves to act like drunkards with clumsy, imprecise gestures as a means of causing the adversary to relax his guard. They then take advantage of this, to the surprise of all, to land a completely unexpected blow.

By the same token, Miyamoto Musashi—this most illustrious of all samurai died in bed even though he took part in over 60 duels (sometimes one against ten)—provides valuable advice on this subject in his *Book of Five Rings*. For example, he explains: "Everything obeys a phenomenon of transmission. Sleep is contagious, so is a yawn. . . . When your adversaries are still in the grip of excitement and rushing at you, adopt the opposite approach with a nonchalant attitude as if you were completely indifferent. They will be contaminated by this and relax their guard. This is the moment to launch an energetic and rapid attack."

Many great masters of *budo* have concealed themselves under the guise of being inoffensive individuals, not so they can better surprise possible aggressors, but primarily so they avoid popularity and the curiosity of others. Some have even preferred humiliation and being mistaken for cowards than to responding to senseless provocations. Respectful of all life, they only fight when there is no other choice.

To discover a master is not always an easy task, and many have occasionally crossed paths with a great one unknowingly. Blinded at first glance by their apparent insignificance, most people have thereby proven their inability to see past appearances. But is not the principal enemy and the primary reason we stumble into the snare of appearances basically identical with the deeply rooted illusions that we nurture within?

Satisfied with their physical strength, their technical prowess, and their relative agility, many practitioners and even a few experts feel they have achieved a high level of proficiency, if not mastery. Confident they have achieved their goal and have nothing left to learn, they stop progressing and thereby lose any chance they might have had of achieving true proficiency, which, far from disappearing with age, grows stronger with every passing day.

Here are two proverbs:

*A footprint is left by a sandal, but is the footprint the sandal?*

*To the ignorant, a precious stone looks like a simple pebble.*

## The Old Warrior's Wager

One day Lord Naoshige declared to one of his older samurai, Shimomura Shoun, "The strength and vitality of that young Katshushige are admirable for one of his age. When he spars with his companions he even beats the oldest among them."

"Even though I may no longer be a young man myself," said the old Shoun, "I am willing to bet that he won't be able to defeat me."

Naoshige was more than delighted to arrange the match that took place that very evening in his castle's courtyard, in the midst of a large number of samurai. They were eager to see what would happen to that old joker Shoun.

At the outset of the match the young and powerful Katsushige rushed at his frail adversary and grabbed him tightly, determined not to waste any time putting him in his place. Several times Shoun left the ground and tumbled in the dust but, to everyone's surprise, managed to find his balance each time at the last possible moment. Exasperated, the young man tried again to hurl him down with all his might, but this time Shoun skillfully took advantage of his adversary's movement, and it was he who managed to unbalance Katshushige and knock him to the ground.

After aiding his dazed foe back to his feet, Shoun approached Lord Naoshige to say, "To be proud of one's strength when one has not yet mastered one's passion is like bragging about one's faults in public."

## The Law of Balance

Having the opportunity to stay in Japan at the beginning of the century, a European decided to learn *jiujutsu*, since it appeared to be a most formidable kind of combat skill. He began study under a renowned master.

But imagine his surprise when, after three lessons, he had still not learned any combat techniques! He had only learned exercises consisting of very slow and relaxed movements. At the end of the third lesson he decided to go find his master.

"Sir, since the time I've come here I've done nothing

that has any resemblance to combat exercises."

"Sit down, I beg you," responded the master.

The European casually settled down on the tatami and the master sat down facing him.

"When are you going to start teaching me *jiujutsu*?"

The master smiled and asked, "Are you well seated?"

"I don't know. Is there a good way to sit?"

For an answer, his master simply pointed at how he himself was sitting, his back perfectly straight, his head a perfect extension of his spinal column.

"But listen," the European shot back, "I didn't come here to learn how to sit."

" I know," said the master patiently, "I know. You want to learn how to fight. But how can you fight if you can't find your balance?"

"I don't really see what sitting down has to do with combat."

"If you can't keep your balance when you are seated, that is, in the simplest of postures, how do you expect to keep your balance in other circumstances life will throw at you, especially combat?"

Leaning toward his perplexed foreign student, the Japanese man lightly pushed him. The European fell over backwards. The master, still seated, then asked his student to try and knock him over. First the student timidly pushed with one hand, then using both, he tried vigorously to push his master, with no success. All at once, the master moved slightly and the other went flying forward, sprawled face first upon the tatami.

With the barest hint of a smile, the master added, "I hope you are beginning to grasp the importance of balance."

## The Dreadful Secret of the Little Bonze

A Chinese bonze by the name of Chen Yuan Pin had moved to the Edo (Tokyo) region around 1650. He had crossed the western sea to teach calligraphy and poetry. Having found a quiet refuge in an outbuilding of the Kokushoji temple, he lived alone and was only seen during the times he taught lessons. With the discretion of a cat, and as tranquil as the surface of a pond, the old monk seemed to be as fragile as a jade lamp.

Poems flowered from his mouth like lotus blooms, the brush danced in his agile fingers, engendering harmony. Chen Yuan Pin's merits soon earned the appreciation of the shogun who took the monk into his service. The monk taught his art to the young nobles and dignitaries of the court, but he obstinately refused to move into the palace, preferring the silence of his retreat to the tumultuous life of the court. Often, when returning to the palace, the old monk crossed the path of rough samurai who eyed him disdainfully. In lowered voices they accused this protégé of the shogun of softening the spirit of the young nobles destined for the life of warriors. One does not win a battle with a brush in one's hand, or by shouting poems from a head that is overcrammed with philosophy! Discreet as a cat, tranquil as the surface of a pond, fragile as a jade lamp, Chen Yuan Pin continued on his way, his face lit by an imperturbable smile.

One evening, after he had remained quite late at the palace teaching, the old monk started back to the Kokushoji temple, located far from town, escorted by three guards he had finally agreed to accept after giving in to the alarmed personal pleas of the shogun. After leaving town, the path plunged almost immediately into deep woods. All at once a band of brigands surged out of the trees, surrounding Chen Yuan Pin and his escort. Their battle raged savagely. The three guards battled back desperately and a dance of death unfolded around the old monk. Superior in number, the brigands prevailed over the courage of the three samurai who found themselves disarmed and about to die in the furious mêlée. Then, in a way that was as sudden as it was unexpected, Chen Yuan Pin went on the attack. Swift as lightning, flexible as a reed, ungraspable like the wind, his hands, feet, and elbows transformed themselves into dreadful weapons. Four brigands thudded heavily to the ground, taken out of action. The others, frightened by the peaceful monk's terrifying metamorphosis, took to their heels. They fled as fast and as far as they could, as if they had just seen a *kami* or some other supernatural being.

Full of admiration, the three samurai pulled themselves together and set off again on the path that brought the bonze back to the temple. On the way, no longer holding themselves back, they asked Chen Pin to tell them his secret, the dreadful secret of his strength. The monk kept his silence and continued on to the temple, discreet as a cat, tranquil as the surface of a pond, and fragile as a jade lamp. On arrival at the temple, he said farewell to the guards and retired for the night. The three samurai, determined to learn more about this monk's mysterious combat ability, kept watch at the door of the temple until dawn.

The next day they renewed their pleas to the old monk, begging him to accept them as students, or even as simple servants.

"My art is for well-tempered souls. The path of knowledge is long and steep," the bonze told them.

"We are ready for anything," replied the three guards.

The old bonze accepted them as students and over many long years initiated them into the art of *wu shu,* the perfect art, that he had learned in the Middle Kingdom. Outside of their common apprenticeship, each student specialized in one of the branches of *wu shu.* One of them achieved mastery in the science of strikes, the second in that of grips and strangleholds, and the third in that of *atemis,* the blows to vital points.

After numerous years of intensive training and having begun to integrate the secret of Chen Yuan Pin, the hour had come for the three students to leave their aged master. They were now obliged to pass on what they had received, each in their own special discipline. On the day of their departure, Chen Yuan Pin gave them some final advice and reminded them only to teach those ready to follow the way of the heart. The master gave them all his blessing, then retired to the temple, discreet as a cat, tranquil as the surface of a pond, and, under the weight of his years, even more fragile than a jade lamp, with his face made radiant by his peaceful smile.

## The Champion and the Master

Umedzu was the fencing champion of his province. On learning that the famous master Toda Seigen was passing through the town in which he taught, Umedzu was eager to see how he measured up to him.

When Seigen was asked if he accepted the challenge the champion of the province had given him, he responded, "Absolutely not. I see no reason whatsoever to fight with this man as I have nothing to prove. Tell him that a sword fight is a matter of life and death, and I cannot lightly assume such risks."

Taking this response to be an excuse from Seigen, who apparently feared being defeated and losing his reputation, Umedzu let the master's refusal to fight become public knowledge and did not hesitate to treat him as a coward.

The lord of the province caught wind of the matter and took an intense interest in it, as he himself was a passionate fan of fencing. He had a message brought to Seigen in which he courteously pleaded with him to accept the match. Seigen refused to respond. The request was sent three times, each time in a more insistent tone.

Seigen could not continue to refuse any longer without

infringing upon the rules and obligations of the samurai, who are expected to show obedience toward feudal authority. He resolved then to fight Umedzu. The arbitrator, the place, and the date of the match were thereupon quickly decided.

Determined to make sure everything weighed in his favor, Umedzu quickly made his way to a Shinto sanctuary. He spent three days and nights there performing a religious purification ritual as a means of preparing for the upcoming combat and propitiating his gods.

Someone told Seigen all the details of his adversary's preparation and advised him that he do likewise. But the master only smiled serenely and replied, "I try to cultivate sincerity in my heart and inner harmony at every instant. These are not things that the gods can give me at critical moments."

As had been previously arranged, the two combatants met at the site selected for their match. The provincial lord came in person with a large part of his retinue to witness at this long awaited meeting. Accompanied by a crowd of students and admirers, Umedzu carried a *boken,* a wooden sword more than a yard in length. Seigen, on the other hand, carried only a small club that was barely over a foot long. On seeing this, Umedzu turned to the arbitrator to demand that his adversary also be given a regulation-sized *boken.* He didn't want his victory to be attributed in any way to the ridiculous weapon carried by his opponent! The demand was transmitted to Seigen who refused, saying that he was perfectly happy with his little piece of wood. The arbitrator eventually decided that each could keep their respective weapons.

Umedzu leapt furiously into battle with vigorous and re-peated attacks. He jumped and roared like a ferocious ani-mal. His weapon hammered down at his opponent with dreadful precision and sliced at him with prodigious speed.

Almost nonchalantly, Master Seigen evaded each of these blows with the flexibility and grace of a cat. His utterly indif-ferent gaze never left the eyes of his opponent for even a sec-ond and his totally relaxed body appeared to be playing, even dancing, with the sword that brushed by him in alarming fash-ion. Umedzu, beside himself, was wielding his *boken* with all his might and raged at finding no target but empty space.

This fascinating ballet could not last for long though. All at once, for no apparent reason, the champion came to a stand-still. A look of intense pain could be read in his face. The small cudgel of the master had certainly scored a hit upon him, but no one could have said exactly where. Seigen took advantage of this to seize his adversary's *boken*. He threw it as far as he could and made ready to leave the area of the match and Umedzu alone with his crushing defeat. But the latter, in a fit of rage, drew the dagger he wore at his belt and rushed toward the master.

In a barely perceptible movement, Seigen's little cudgel whistled through the air. It struck his opponent for a second time, but on this occasion Umedzu collapsed in a heap on the ground.

## A Time Bomb

An expert in Chinese boxing had settled in a remote village and had been living there for several weeks. He was beginning to find his situation there quite pleasing as the fear he inspired among the peasants permitted him to act as if he were lord of the area. What he found especially gratifying was that no one there dared resist him or cross his path in anyway, until the day, that is, when a little old man with a white beard did not step out of his way, and instead, continued walking straight toward him. In conformity with his usual behavior, the expert attempted to bully the old man and jostle him off the path, but found himself lunging into thin air because the elder man had dodged his shove. Furious, the boxer pounced on the old man to give him a good pummeling. In the ensuing mêlée, the old man clumsily attempted to block these punches and even managed to land a soft punch to the brute's chest. But clearly having the disadvantage of weight in this bout, he was eventually sent rolling into the dust. Satisfied with the correction he had just administered, the champion left by the roadside the inanimate body of the old, impertinent fool who had dared resist him. As soon as the brute had vanished into the distance, the little old man opened one eye, then the other, got back up, shook the dust off his clothes, and peacefully left the village.

With each passing day, the boxer felt more and more ill.

His body grew weaker, his respiration and digestion became difficult, and he had frequent headaches.

The day arrived when he finally had to take to his bed shivering with fever. He no longer had the strength to move, and he could barely even find enough energy to speak.

After giving long consideration to the possible reasons for his condition, he found but one plausible explanation: the light blow that the old man gave him had obviously touched a vital point, and its effects had occurred with a delayed reaction. Finally realizing that it was the old man who given him this lesson, he understood how deceptive appearances could be and how he had been living, until then, blinded by the illusion of his strength. Overcome by true remorse, he sent people in search of the old man to ask his pardon for his unspeakable behavior and to thank him for having forced him to open his eyes.

The little old man, who lived in a hermitage close to the village, did not delay his arrival. Touched by the thug's sincere repentance, he decided to heal him personally. After several sessions of shiatsu (digital acupuncture) and treatment with medicinal plants, the young man was put back on his feet. Infused with a genuine need for learning, he humbly requested the old hermit to accept him as a student.

He remained in the hermitage until the death of his master, and, when he went back down into the village, his presence no longer inspired fear, but feelings of calm and respect.

# 5

# The Great Test

*Beneath the sword raised high*
*Hell makes you tremble*
*But by confronting it*
*You discover the land of bliss."*

## MIYAMOTO MUSASHI,
### Book of Five Rings

The martial arts practitioner is soon confronted by a crucial problem: fear. Training bouts, although most often conducted in a spirit of friendly competition, are not without risk. One who has been at the receiving end of some hard blows will likely feel apprehensive about further engagement, and experience the paralyzing effects of fear: the body contracts, internal energy ceases circulating, reactions become uncontrolled. In the grip of this negative emotion, it is no longer possible to view the situation clearly, and, for that reason, to confront it adequately. In the case of real danger, the consequences can be dramatic. As long as a man can be possessed by fear, he cannot attain true mastery. Freeing oneself from fear is a decisive step on the path.

Samurai, whose fate was to risk their lives on a daily basis, were forced to find a rapid solution to this problem. If they were terror-stricken on the battlefield, any possibility of confronting the enemy effectively was doomed to failure. For this reason, General Kenshin, a Zen adept, had the habit of telling his troops: "Enter combat firmly convinced of victory and you will return home safe and sound. Engage in battle completely determined to die, and you will live, because those who cling desperately to life, die, and those who defy death, live."

A maxim of *jiujutsu* expresses this same idea in other terms: "Those who hang on will certainly fall, those who don't cling need have no fear of falling."

This is easy enough to say, but oh, how difficult to achieve. It does seem, however, that in desperate cases, such as when life is at stake, people are capable of astounding things. This is known as the "self-preservation instinct." Ordinary individuals utilize very little of their true potential in everyday life, but faced with a sudden danger they react with a strength or speed they didn't even know they had. An old man will make a prodigious leap to avoid being crushed; a woman will manage to lift an enormous weight to save her child.

Everything happens quickly in a life-threatening situation; there is no room for the superfluous. Every fraction of a second counts, and one must be entirely present in the here and now. Psychological and emotional barriers vanish so as to make room for the intervention of a higher energy that leads the individual to give profoundly of him- or herself. But once the danger has passed and the threat has been removed, the ordinary individual reclaims his or her "rights." Fear can again make its appearance, often in response to a trifle. Man again finds his problems where and just as he left them, and he is no longer capable of dealing with them effectively because he cannot turn on his self-preservation instinct at will.

Yet the masters declare it is possible to liberate oneself from fear. To do so it is indispensable to look at it steadfastly and trace it to its source. If and when the source of one's fear is discovered, it will evaporate like a puff of smoke, like a nightmare dissipating upon awakening.

## The Fissure

The students of Kenkichi Sakakibara, who taught the art of the sword, were beginning to wonder seriously if their master had gone mad. For over a month he had been regularly devoting himself to a singular task: attempting to split a steel helmet with one blow of his sword. All his attempts had been futile, as his blade would either bounce back, bend, or break on the helmet, which remained stubbornly intact.

Sakakibara didn't really know if anyone was truly capable of performing this feat. The samurai helmet was in fact manufactured from steel of a superior quality and no weapon could actually pierce it. Even musket balls would simply ricochet off of it. On the other hand, it was true that martial epics reported that the heroes of olden days were capable of splitting a helmet with but one blow of a sword. In memory of them, the ceremony of *kabuto wari* (the helmet stroke) took place before the emperor every year. Sakakibara's students were unaware that their master had been personally invited to participate in this ceremony.

On the eve of the ceremony, Sakakibara still hadn't succeeded in cutting the helmet. His despair was boundless because he believed failing this test would earn him the dishonor of having betrayed the emperor's confidence in him.

Sick at heart, he went to the imperial palace for the ceremony of *kabuto wari*. The greatest champions of the land had all been invited. Each took their turn. The helmet remained intact and showed not a trace of their assaults against it. On the other hand, a good number of blades had been broken in the attempt.

The only champion remaining to perform the ceremony was none other than Sakakibara. When his turn came, he knelt before the emperor, striving to conceal his disarray, and greeted him respectfully. He then approached the helmet, remaining motionless, sword in hand. Everything now rested upon him, the last contestant; he was the emperor's last possible hope for a successful outcome. Aware that his normal strength was not enough for the task at hand, he tried to concentrate on his maximum potential. But nothing happened. He felt completely at a loss and empty.

It was at this moment that something gave way and opened within. A mysterious energy, an irresistible *ki*, spread throughout his being. What happened next occurred as if by magic. He slowly raised his sword above his head before slashing it back down with the speed of lightning. At the very same moment a *kiai* that echoed like a crack of thunder sprang from the very depths of his being.

The helmet did not move, and the sword remained intact. When the judge examined the helmet closely, he observed a cut some five inches in length.

Why did Sakakibara succeed where so many before him had failed? Perhaps, some said, it was because he had decided to perform *seppuku* (ritual suicide by hara-kiri), if he failed.

## In the Hands of Fate

A great general by the name of Nobunaga had made the decision to attack the enemy even though his own troops were quite inferior in number. He himself was confident of victory, but his soldiers didn't exactly share his faith. While on their way to meet the enemy, Nobunaga stopped in front of a Shinto shrine and told his warriors, "I am going to meditate and ask for aid from the *kami*. Then I will throw a coin. If it is heads, we will win, but if it is tails, we will lose. We are in the hands of fate."

After having gathered his thoughts and meditated for several moments, Nobunaga emerged from the temple and tossed a coin. It was heads. His soldiers' morale was inflated as high as it could go. The troops, firmly convinced of emerging victorious, fought with such extraordinary fear-lessness that they quickly won the battle.

After the victory, the general's aide-de-camp said to him, "Nobody can change fate. This unlooked for victory is new proof of that."

"Who really knows?" Nobunaga replied, showing him a fake coin with heads on each side.

## The Condemned Man

During the Japanese feudal period, a man belonging to the servant class took the imprudent step of causing trouble for a very influential politician. This dignitary then demanded that his master hand him over, an action that, of course, would be the equivalent of sealing the servant's death warrant. His master was in no position to reject this request, which had all the trappings of an official command.

All the same, the master suggested to his servant: "I am truly distressed at having to turn you over to this official who will no doubt punish you with death. I am in no posi-tion to do very much to help you except to propose this par-ticular expedient: Take a sword and fight a duel with me. If you kill me you will be free to flee. If you lose, you will at least not have died as a criminal, but in combat like a warrior."

His servant replied: "That would be insane. You are an acknowledged fencing expert and a renowned teacher of swordsmanship. How would I, who have almost never held a weapon in my life, have any prayer of defeating you?"

The master secretly harbored a desire to fight with someone whose last hope of staying alive was gone. He insisted: "What difference will it make? What have you got to lose? Take your chances and let me see what I am able to do."

The servant eventually yielded to his master's entreaties and accepted the match. The two men then met face-to-face, swords in hand, to duel to the death.

Very quickly the master found himself in a desperate position. The servant, unleashed, had attacked with total abandon and thrown himself wholeheartedly into the battle. Forced to retreat step-by-step, the master was finally trapped in a corner, his back to the wall. There was not a minute to lose, as he was on the verge of being utterly overwhelmed. Gathering together all his energy, the master let out a shout and gave his adversary a terrible blow with his sword.

Later, the master confessed to his students: "What a desperate fight that was. Truly, I should have been defeated by my servant. I sincerely hope that none of you ever have to fight someone who has been condemned to death and thus has nothing left to lose. Taking into account what this poor, inexperienced wretch was capable of, just imagine what it would have been like facing a high-level expert!"

One of the students asked: "When you landed a blow on your servant, was it because you had found a flaw in his concentration?"

"There wasn't a single flaw, and it is purely a miracle that my sword touched him. The *kiai* I yelled may have played some role in my victory."

## A Master with no Technique

The great sword master Tajima no Kami was the personal teacher of this art to the shogun (the imperial ruler). One day one of the shogun's personal guards came to him for instruction in the handling of his sword.

"As far as I can tell," said Tajima, "you are yourself a master of this art. Tell me, I beg you, what school you are from."

The guard answered: "I am truly sorry to have to tell you that I never studied in a school."

"Are you making fun of me? Don't try to tell me such lies. I know what I'm saying and I have great experience in judging people."

"I regret being the one to call your reputation into question, but I swear to you that I have never learned the handling of a sword under the direction of any master, and that moreover, I must confess that I don't know a great deal about this art. I have a great need for a technical apprenticeship."

The visitor's assurance and genuinely honest air caused the master to reconsider for a moment. He then said: "Since you have said it is true, then it surely must be. But I still think you must have been a master in something. I can't say just what."

"Very well. Since you insist, I will tell you this much. When I was a child the idea came to me that when I was a samurai I would not under any circumstances entertain the fear of death, and since that time I have never ceased, over all those years, to seek contact with the idea of death. Today the fear has completely ceased to concern me. I have mastered it, in a certain sense. Could that perhaps be the mastery you are thinking of?"

"Precisely!" exclaimed Tajima no Kami, "That is exactly what I was trying to say. I am happy to find I wasn't fooled. To be free of the fear of death is one of the most important secrets in the art of the sword. I have trained hundreds of students, but few among them have truly attained that degree of mastery. In your case, you no longer have any need for technical training of any sort. You are already a master."

### The Tea Master and the Ronin

The lord of Tosa had gone to Edo, the capital, to make an official visit to the shogun. He could not bear to go without his master of *cha no yu,* of whom he was extremely proud. The *cha no yu* or tea ceremony is a Japanese art that has a strong Zen influence. Every gesture must be performed with a great deal of concentration. It is a matter of tasting the mystery of the "here and now," thanks to a very delicate ritual.

In order to gain admittance into the palace, the master of

the tea ceremony had to dress in traditional samurai attire, including the two swords that is that uniform's most distinctive feature. Since his arrival in Edo, the *cha no yu* specialist had not set foot out of the palace. Several times a day he performed his art in his lord's apartment, to the great pleasure of those invited there. He even presided in the presence of the shogun himself. One day, his lord gave him permission to go out and wander about the city. Seizing this opportunity to visit the capital, the tea ceremony master, still dressed as a samurai, ventured out into the crowded, busy streets of Edo. While crossing a bridge he was suddenly bumped by a *ronin*, one of those wandering warriors who can be either the most gallant of knights or the most arrogant of brigands. This one had the air of being one of the worst sort. He stated in a cold tone: "So, you are a Tosa samurai. I don't appreciate being bumped aside by the likes of you; I think we need to settle this little matter by the sword."

In desperation the tea ceremony master confessed the truth: "I am not a real samurai, despite appearances. I am only a humble specialist in *cha no yu* who knows absolutely nothing about wielding a sword."

The *ronin* had no desire whatsoever to believe this story, especially as his real motive was to steal some money from his victim, whose timid character he had sensed. He remained unyielding in his demands and raised his voice to further impress his listener. A crowd quickly formed around the two men. Profiting from this stroke of good fortune, the *ronin* threatened to publicly declare that a Tosa samurai was a coward and was scared to fight.

Seeing that it was impossible to make the *ronin* see reason, and fearing that his conduct would bring shame to his lordship's honor, the tea ceremony master accepted the duel out of principle and resigned himself to dying. But, not wanting to die passively and give people cause to say that Tosa samurai didn't know how to fight, he had an idea. Recalling that he had passed a sword school several minutes before, he thought he could at least learn there how to hold a sword correctly and face his inevitable death honorably. He explained this to the *ronin:* "As I am running an errand for my lord, I must first fulfill my duty. This could yet take another two hours. Do you have the patience to wait for me here?"

Either out of chivalrous respect for the rules of *bushido,* or imagining that his victim needed this time to put together an impressive amount of money, the *ronin* agreed to this delay.

The *cha no yu* master rushed off to the school he had noticed earlier and asked to see the master immediately on a matter of great urgency. The doorkeeper was little inclined to allow entrance to this strange visitor who did not appear to be in his right mind and did not carry any letter of recommendation. But, touched by the man's tormented expression, he finally decided to bring him to his master. The sword instructor listened with great interest to his visitor's retelling of his misadventure and his desire to die as a samurai.

"This is truly a remarkable, even unique case," said the master.

"This is no time to joke," his visitor replied.

"I'm not joking at all, I assure you. You are truly an exception. Customarily students who come to see me wish to learn how to wield a sword and how to win. You, on the other hand, want me to teach you the art of dying. But first, couldn't you serve me a cup of tea in that you are a master of that incomparable art?"

The visitor didn't complain as this was certainly his last opportunity to perform his art. Appearing to completely forget his tragic fate, he carefully prepared the tea, then served it with surprising calm and presence of mind. He performed each gesture as if nothing else had any importance at that moment.

Having observed him attentively throughout the entire ceremony, the sword master was profoundly impressed by his visitor's degree of concentration.

"Excellent!" he cried out, "Excellent! The level of self-mastery you have attained by practicing your art is sufficient to allow you to act with dignity before any samurai. You have everything that is required for a death with honor, don't worry. Please just listen to a few pieces of advice. When you see your *ronin*, think as if you were about to serve tea to a friend. After a polite greeting, thank him for granting you the delay. Next delicately fold your jacket and place it on the ground, with your fan on top, just as you would for the tea ceremony. Place the headband signifying your resolution around your forehead, roll up your sleeves, then announce to your adversary that you are ready for the duel. After drawing your sword from its scabbard, raise it above your head while closing your eyes. All that will be left for you to do is to concentrate to your fullest extent so as to be ready to vigorously lower your weapon at the very moment you hear the *ronin* utter his battle cry. I wager this will result in both your deaths."

The visitor thanked the master for his valuable advice and returned at the appointed time to the spot near the bridge where the *ronin* awaited him. Following the instructions he had been given, the *cha no yu* master prepared for combat just as he would if he were about to offer a cup of tea to a guest. When he raised his sword and closed his eyes, his adversary's face changed expression. The *ronin* could hardly believe his eyes.

Could this man who was now facing him really be the same man he had challenged?

In a state of extreme concentration, the tea ceremony master awaited the shout that would be the signal for his very last movement, his ultimate action. But after several minutes (that seemed to him like hours) had gone by, no cry had yet been uttered. No longer able to restrain himself, the impromptu samurai opened his eyes.

No one was there. There was no longer anybody facing him.

The *ronin,* not knowing how to attack this formidable

opponent who revealed not a single flaw in his concentration, nor the slightest trace of fear in his bearing, had backed
away step-by-step until he was out of sight, no longer seeking compensation and quite thankful of having gotten away
with his skin intact.

## At the Edge of the Abyss

A mob had formed in the village square to admire the talent
of a renowned archer. During his demonstration he had performed some tricks of skill that attested to his great proficiency in this art. For example, he was able to shoot several
arrows in succession while holding a water-filled cup perfectly balanced on his forearm.

Each exploit had been applauded enthusiastically by the
crowd. But the archer was disturbed to note that a man in
the first row of spectators had not shown the slightest bit of
admiration from the very beginning of the demonstration.
He could not stop himself from challenging this onlooker
and asking him why. A murmur ran through the crowd, as
the man in question was clearly a Taoist adept, thus a powerful magician in the popular imagination. What kind of
trick would he play?

The Taoist contented himself by replying: "Your skill with
the bow is not bad technically, but you are far from being
able to shoot without shooting."

The archer told himself that this was a perfect example of Taoist-speak—hermetic and obscure, and just another way, like so many others, to make a speaker seem interesting. All the same he dared to demand an explanation. "What exactly do you mean by this story of shooting without shooting?"

"If we were balanced on a rock overhanging a precipice that plunged steeply for more than three hundred yards, would you still be able to shoot as well?"

The archer accepted the dare. He followed the Taoist into the mountains where the adept scaled a boulder and advanced along the edge of an abyss that was more than one hundred yards deep. Then he turned and walked backward until two-thirds the length of both his feet extended over the rock and thus into thin air. Then, grasping the hand of the famous archer, he pulled him toward him. The archer resisted with all his strength until he eventually was lying flat on his stomach in order to have a better grip on the rock. Covered with sweat from head to toe, he hardly dared to move.

After allowing him enough time to get a handle on his emotions, the Taoist said to him: "The accomplished man leaps into the azure vastness of heaven, or plunges into the whirlpools of yellow springs, or even adventures beyond the eight borders of this world without showing the slightest sign of alarm. And you, although tightly clinging to a rock, are still trembling, and your body is paralyzed with fear. How can you expect to hit the target under these conditions?"

# 6

## Lessons of the Zen Masters

*Walking is also Zen.*
*Whether one moves or remains still,*
*The body remains constantly at peace.*
*Even if one finds oneself facing a sword,*
*The mind remains tranquil.*

### SHODOKA,
### The Chant of the Immediate Satori

Hojo Tokimune, the *shiken* (regent) who repelled the Mongol invasions in the thirteenth century, is among the greatest warriors and heads of state in Japanese history. He was also one of the first to study under the guidance of Zen masters and promoted the development of this Buddhist offshoot. Legend says that he visited the famous Zen master Bukko one day to ask him, "How can I escape from the monster of fear, which is the worst enemy one can face in this life?"

"Suppress the fear at its source," was Bukko's reply.

"But where does it come from?"

"It comes from Tokimune himself."

"But fear is what I detest above all else. How could it come from me?" Tokimune exclaimed.

"Try to throw overboard your adored 'me' called Tokimune and then examine your feelings. I will consent to see you again after you have done that."

"How am I supposed to do that?" Tokimune persisted.

"Silence your thoughts."

"How is that possible?"

"Seat yourself in the cross-legged position of meditation and look at what you imagine belongs to Tokimune in the source of your thoughts."

"I have a public life that is so busy it is difficult to find any free time for meditating."

"Whatever the activities you find yourself engaged in, take them as opportunities for your inner seeking and one day you will discover just who your dear Tokimune is."

Tokimune's thought process is not exceptional in Japanese history. Numerous warriors of all ranks became initiated into Zen. Among the greatest generals of the fourteenth century are the Zen adepts Kenshin and Shingen. The famous sword master Tajima no Kami was the disciple of the abbot Takuan. Warriors of much more modest reputation, even *ronin,* frequented Zen monasteries.

What did Zen have that attracted such fierce samurai?

The virile attitude exhibited by Zen masters was certainly the deciding factor in this attraction. Showing proof of the greatest cold-bloodedness, the Zen masters never betrayed any weakness even in the most dramatic of situations. Nothing seemed to rattle them, not even death. "When one's thoughts are tamed, fire itself seems cool and refreshing," were the last words of the abbot Kweisen, just before he was burned alive in his monastery, which was set ablaze when he refused to turn it over to a besieging army.

The warriors were also seduced by Zen's essentially practical methodology, which rejected any dogmatic, ritual, or intellectual formalism. Zen is neither philosophy nor religion; it is a way that leads to a decisive experience: *satori*. *Satori* is the awakening of illumination about one's self and reality.

The word *zen* derives from the Chinese *chan*, which itself is derived from the Sanskrit word *dhyana*, the meaning of which is "meditation," "contemplation." "In its essence, Zen is the art of seeing into the very nature of being. It indicates the way that leads from slavery to liberation. By allowing us to drink directly from the source of life, it frees us from the yokes under which we, as finite beings, suffer continuously," is Zen scholar D. T. Suzuki's explanation. Zen holds the key to liberation and self-realization. Man can then become master of the latent energies that dwell within.

As a guide to the student, the master transmits techniques and advice. His very presence is a valuable aid. But his role stops there. It is the disciple himself who will have to perform the work necessary to achieve awakening. *Satori* can only emerge after the clouds of ignorance and illusion have been scattered. It is, in fact, a matter of going beyond the reality-distorting dualism manufactured by the intellect.

In addition to seated meditation *(zazen)*, which is an internal exploration of the depths of one's being and the cosmos, Zen teaches techniques designed to provoke realizations that are capable of shattering "the mind's boundaries." To illustrate this concept there are dialogues *(mondo)* between masters and their disciples. To the question, "What is Zen?" the master may sometimes answer: "What are you?" or even something like, "The cypress stands in the cemetery," if he doesn't just simply shrug his shoulders.

Zen koans are a kind of puzzle or rebus. They are illogical questions that have no reasonable answer upon which the disciple is expected to meditate. Some of the more well-known ones include: "Everything returns to the One but where does the One return?" and "When you clap your two hands, a certain sound is made. What is the sound of one hand clapping?"

Far from being cut off from reality, Zen is actually an art of living that allows one to be fully present in every gesture of daily life. To achieve their internal realizations, Zen monks personally performed the manual tasks necessary for the upkeep of their monasteries and practiced traditional crafts. For them these were opportunities to practice "meditation in action," to maintain concentration in movement. For that reason numerous Zen masters practiced and continue to practice martial arts in order to realize "a closer union between man and instrument, subject and object, act and actor, mind and body." A Zen master is not only someone capable of remaining for hours in *zazen*, but is primarily one capable of harmoniously mastering all levels of existence as well. Mastering an art is proof of an inner realization.

While Zen and the martial arts are intimately linked to Japan, the ancient national religion, Shinto, remains the backdrop of *budo*. The Shinto altar and Shinto ceremonies have their place in every traditional *dojo*. Master Ueshiba, for example, followed a course of instruction of Shinto origin under the guidance of the priest Degushi.

Taoism is the traditional way of the Middle Kingdom. Zen itself is a synthesis of Indian Buddhism and Taoism. A veritable internal alchemy, Taoist teaching goes through a series of techniques that lead to the awakening of latent energies, with an eye to the revitalization of the adept. The methods used are quite similar to those found in Zen: meditation, breath control, enigmatic questions and answers, and, of course, the practice of moving meditation, the maintaining of concentration in simple everyday actions. To the Taoists, meditation during activity is a thousand times superior to meditation when resting: "It is only when serenity has been established in movement that the universal rhythm reveals itself."

Cultivated by Taoist masters, tai chi chuan represents one of the most refined of all the martial arts. It is simultaneously a form of combat, therapy, symbolic dance, and physical meditation. As its name indicates, this art governs the energy's action within the body. The masters state that it is necessary "to conserve the original *chi* since it maintains both the purity of heaven and the serenity of the earth; it permits the realization of a man."

While the means of access are many and varied, the martial arts masters were capable of integrating into their practice those disciplines that could lead to the ultimate secret.

*The Great Way has no gate;*
*Thousands of roads flow into it.*
*The one who crosses through this gateless gate,*
*Walks freely between Heaven and Earth.*

### At the Gates of Heaven

One day a samurai came to see the Zen master Hakuin and asked him, "Is there truly a heaven and a hell?"

"Who are you?" the master asked.

"I am the samurai . . ."

"You, a soldier!" Hakuin exclaimed. "Just look at yourself. What lord would want you in his service? You look like a beggar."

The samurai grew angry and drew his sword. Hakuin continued: "Oh, good, you even have a sword! But you are certainly too clumsy to cut off my head with it."

Losing all self-control, the samurai raised his sword, ready to strike the master. At that very moment the latter spoke, saying, "Here is where the gates to hell open."

Surprised by the monk's air of calm assurance, the samurai sheathed his sword and bowed before him.

"This is where the gates of heaven open," the master then said.

## From the Hand of the Master

Dokyo Yetan (1641–1721), the most illustrious Zen master of his time, one day received a visit from a *ken-jutsu* teacher who told him, "From the time I was a young child, I have practiced the art of the sword, having trained intensively under the guidance of several masters. I have been successful in perfectly integrating the styles of the most famous schools. But despite all my efforts to get there, I have yet to attain the point of supreme realization. Could you give me any advice on what method I should choose?" The Zen master stood up, approached his visitor, and asked him in a whisper to give him all of his attention so that he wouldn't miss a detail of what he was about to confide to him. The man therefore leaned forward to extend his ear, which received a magisterial slap from Dokyo Yetan's hand. The master then let loose with a powerful kick. Before he even knew what was happening, the sword instructor lost his balance and the impact of his sudden contact with the floor gave him, it seemed, *satori,* a spiritual awakening.

It has to be believed that this was a decisive moment in the visitor's life, for he didn't delay in becoming an acclaimed master himself shortly thereafter. His remarkable development, obvious to all those who practiced his art, intrigued more than one warrior. Most among those who asked him what his secret was remained incredulous when he admitted to them that it resided in the very special method of the monk Dokyo Yetan. Several, however, decided to go see for themselves. Their voyage wasn't a disappointment, as can be seen in the tale that follows.

Three high-ranking samurai had invited Dokyo Yetan to come drink a cup of tea with them. They questioned him extensively about Zen, but because the master responded in a very enigmatic fashion, one of the samurai, somewhat overwrought, pushed forward to say, "You are certainly a great master of Zen and we are not in anyway equipped to argue with you on this subject. But if the question of the concentration necessary for fighting were brought up, I am afraid you would be incapable of beating us."

"I wouldn't be so sure if I were you. You see, life has shown me on more than one occasion that one should never form a conclusion before experimenting," the monk replied.

"You would truly allow me to fight a duel with you?" the samurai asked after exchanging an ironic glance with his companions.

"Of course, as that is the only way to verify if what one says is correct."

The warrior picked up a *boken* and handed it to the monk. But the latter refused the weapon saying, "I am a Buddhist and I don't wish to carry an arm, even one made of wood. My fan will serve nicely. Now strike without hesitating. If you succeed in touching me I will admit that you are a great expert."

Convinced he would strike him with his opening blows and fearful of injuring the old monk, the samurai attacked gently, almost in slow motion. But little by little he picked up the pace as his attacks were finding nothing but air. Seeing that the swordsman was exhausting himself in his futile attempts, Dokyo Yetan asked for the duel to be halted and suggested, "What do you say all three of you attack me simultaneously? This would be a splendid exercise for me and give you a chance of besting me."

Struck to the quick in their pride as warriors, the samurai tried to strike the master with every means at their disposal. But he remained untouchable. When he wasn't deflecting the attack with his fan, his body was twisting out of harm's way at the last possible moment. Eventually his three adversaries had to acknowledge that he had defeated them. Convinced not by a long sermon but by this stupefying demonstration, they made the effort to take a much closer look at the true essence of Zen. On their return trip, the young novice who accompanied the master could not stop himself from asking him what his secret was that enabled him so skillfully to evade the sword strokes. Dokyo Yetan explained,

"When right vision is exercised and suffers no impediment, it penetrates everything, including the art of the sword. Ordinary people only concern themselves with words. Once they hear a name, they make a judgment and thus are left clinging to a shadow. But he who is capable of truly seeing views each object in its proper light. On seeing the sword he immediately understands how to face it. He confronts the multiple nature of things and is not confused."

## An Original Form of Conversion

Otsuka Tesshin, although still a young man, had become an expert in wielding a sword. Being also an ambitious young man, he wanted to make a name for himself well beyond the borders of his native province. For this reason he had made up his mind to make a great journey throughout the neighboring lands to see how he measured up to his fellow experts. But before leaving he went to pay his respects to the Zen master Ryuko, the head of a neighboring monastery, whom he knew well. When Ryuko learned of the reason behind this imminent departure he said to young Tesshin, "The world we live in is far larger than you can begin to comprehend. It has to have many men in your profession who are superior to you. The outcome of your adventure could be disastrous." The young man, having made up his mind, showed no signs of reconsidering his decision.

Ryuko continued, "Look at me. I also once desired to be better known in the world. I have practiced meditation here for dozens of years and how many disciples do I have today? We should recognize who we really are and be content with our lot. As the proverb says: "Do not regret being ignored; regret being ignorant.""

This exasperated Tesshin so much that he exclaimed in a fit of passion, "Do you think that my art is of no value? Wielding a sword has nothing at all in common with your discipline. If I leave the town of my birth and challenge someone who has made a big name for himself and defeat him, the event will naturally be reported to his friends and students. If I carry off a number of victories in other regions, my reputation will extend, little by little, throughout the land. Furthermore, I know that I have achieved a good level of mastery in my skill and I have no fear of challenging anyone I chance to meet upon the road before me."

"You would do better to begin with the one in front of you right now. If you manage to defeat me, you can then undertake this long journey across the country. In the event that you lose, however, you must promise to become a monk and be my disciple," the master suggested.

Unable to hold back his laughter, Tesshin responded, "While you surely know all about your Zen, you seem to know nothing about the sword. If you really want to try your luck, all right, I am ready for you."

Ryuko then gave him a bamboo staff and armed himself

with a *hossu* (a wand with a tuft of horse hair on the end, generally carried by Zen masters). Tesshin, sure of himself, tried to score a hit on the master with his bamboo. Despite all his efforts he completely missed his target. Exasperated, he redoubled his efforts. Nothing worked. His strikes continued to hit nothing but air. In contrast, he felt the *hossu* lightly brush over his head during each one of his attempts.

The master ended his demonstration by asking the young man what his thoughts were now.

All Tesshin's boastfulness had vanished. He now humbly acknowledged his defeat. The master wasted no time in immediately requesting his assistants to bring all the necessary implements for shaving Tesshin's head and transforming him into a monk.

### The Test

Masamune, the lord of all the provinces of northeast Japan, was himself a student of Zen. He was seeking a good abbot for the Zen temple that was the resting place for his ancestors' ashes, and a certain monk who lived in an insignificant rural temple was recommended to him. Wishing to test the monk's degree of ability, he invited him to his castle in Sendai. The monk, named Rinan, accepted the invitation and presented himself at Lord Masamune's residence. After entering via a long corridor, the monk was told that the lord awaited him in one of the adjoining rooms. He then opened some sliding doors to enter the room, but no one was there. He crossed through the room and entered into another. Still nobody. Patiently, he headed toward another door. When he opened it, Lord Masamume was waiting to welcome him in decidedly odd fashion: he was poised, sword in hand, ready to strike him. He asked the monk: "What are you thinking of at this very moment, on the border of life and death?"

Rinan didn't give the slightest appearance of being shocked by this odd reception. For his entire answer, he leapt over the sword and struck the unsuspecting Masamune quite a painful blow. The latter, a warlord and master of all the northeast provinces, exclaimed, "This is a dangerous game you are playing!" The monk replied, while giving him a great smack in the back, "What a pretentious man you are!"

## The Archer and the Monk

An archer had been stalking the forest for hours in search of game. He eventually discovered the tracks of a stag and began to follow them. While passing by a sanctuary where a certain Master Ch'an lived, he took advantage of the opportunity to ask the man if he had seen the stag he was tracking go by.

"So, you are a deer hunter," the old monk replied, "tell me, how many can you hit with one arrow?"

"Just one," the hunter answered.

"So you take lots of pains for so little result."

"What are you talking about? Besides, what would you know about shooting a bow?"

"I practice the art of archery myself," the monk declared.

"Since that's the case how many deer can you hit with one arrow," the hunter asked sarcastically.

"The entire herd."

"That's impossible. Don't tell me such lies."

"What do you know about it? But I should tell you that there is a method to achieving this feat."

"Sure there is, and it would be?"

"You must learn to shoot at yourself until you no longer miss."

"I must confess that I cannot begin to imagine how to aim an arrow at myself."

It is said that the hunter, confronted by this apparently insoluble problem, had a sudden awakening, a *satori,* as it is called by the Zen masters, and he decided to follow closely in the monk's footsteps in order to learn how to target his own heart.

# 7

## Winning without Fighting

*He who has mastered the Art doesn't have*
*to use his sword; he compels*
*his adversary to kill himself.*

**TAJIMA NO KAMI**

All the great masters ceaselessly maintained that "the highest mastery is winning without fighting." They believed that their art was meant to protect life, not serve as a method of killing.

For them, nothing could be easier than using their overwhelming superiority to crush an aggressor. Therefore, ridding oneself of an assailant without wounding him is no mean feat. After all, wouldn't true proficiency consist in discouraging or reconciling with a potential adversary? Or, as a Chinese proverb puts it: "An enemy you vanquish remains your enemy. An enemy you convince becomes your friend."

Winning without fighting is not within the scope of just anyone. "An ordinary man will draw his sword if he feels that he has been ridiculed, and risk his very life, but he will not be called a courageous man for doing so. A superior man is never alarmed, even in the most unexpected situations, because he has a great soul and a noble objective," was a favorite saying of Funakoshi Gishin. Someone who cannot control himself when faced with danger runs the risk of becoming aggressive and overreacting violently. In this way he falls right into the hands of his adversary. Sometimes he even sees threats where none are present. The person who remains his own master in all circumstances can confront any situation in total lucidity and with all his means at his disposal. To react violently is an easy solution; the truly clever feat is remaining calm. This is the sentiment expressed by Lao-tsu in one of the famous phrases from the *Tao te Ching*: "Imposing one's will on another is a demonstration of ordinary strength, imposing one's will on oneself attests to true power."

If, despite all his best efforts, a master is dragged into a fight, he will actually try to neutralize his opponent without resorting to combat. The essence of Japanese martial arts is profoundly nonviolent. In fact it is based on the principle of nonresistance, which uses the adversary's own attack to defeat him. The defender, instead of blocking his opponent's movement, dodges it and manipulates it in such a way so as to turn it against the aggressor. If a fighter should push, the defender has only to dodge or pull him to cause him to fall from his own momentum. If the fighter should pull, all one has to do is push. The more powerful the attack, the more disastrous its return effect. The principle of nonresistance causes the attacker to become the victim of his own attack and harvest the fruits of his ill intentions. What could be more just?

The true martial art, whether the Chinese *wu shu* or Japanese *bujutsu,* the "art of stopping the spear," is an excellent application of what Taoist or Zen teachers call *wu-wei.* Generally translated as "non-action," *wu-wei* more precisely means "to let happen," "to act without intervening or resisting." There is a well-known Taoist image: "It is the principle of *wu-wei* that moves all things. Simply because the hub does not move, the wheel turns."

In Eastern tradition, water is the element that best symbolizes *wu-wei* and nonresistance:

*Water opposes no one,*

*And therefore it cannot be confronted.*

*Water gives way to the knife without being cut;*

*It is invulnerable because it doesn't resist.*

## Humor, the Wise Man's Weapon

One evening a small man who was no longer a youngster entered a restaurant in one of the shadiest neighborhoods of Naha, the capital of Okinawa. He had barely crossed the threshold when he was suddenly forced to clench his dorsal muscles against a punch thrown from behind. The small man immediately grabbed his assailant's fist. Twisting it firmly, he calmly dragged his aggressor across the restaurant without even sparing him a glance, then sat down to order a meal and some saki.

After having drunk a few sips from his cup with his free hand, he pulled his assailant before him in order to take a good look at him. After giving him a long stare in which nothing could be read, he freed the man from his gaze saying, "I don't know what you have against me, young man, but what do you say we share a drink?"

This small man, named Itosu, was one of the most renowned karate masters of Okinawa. Funakoshi Gischin studied with him.

Several years after this first episode, Master Itosu was walking down the street late one night and took a terrible punch to his back. Again he had just enough time to contract his muscles and seize the guilty party's hand. Again without turning around, he dragged the desperately struggling thug for several yards.

Clearly alarmed, the young man made fervent excuses and begged the master to excuse his conduct.

The Master then turned around, looked him in the eyes and said: "You are truly unreasonable. You shouldn't be trying to play tricks like that on an old man."

Having said that, he released his young attacker and peacefully resumed his nocturnal promenade.

## The School of Unarmed Combat

The famous master Tsukahara Bokuden was crossing Lake Biwa on a raft with some other travelers. Among them was an extremely pretentious samurai who bragged ceaselessly of his deeds and his mastery of the sword. To hear him talk one would think he was the highest level champion in Japan. At least this was what was assumed by all the other travelers, who listened to him in fearful admiration. All the other travelers but one, that is, for Bokuden remained off to the side and didn't appear to be swallowing these tall tales at all. The samurai noticed this and growing vexed, approached him saying, "I see you also carry a pair of swords. If you are truly a samurai why aren't you saying anything?"

Bokuden replied calmly, "Your remarks have no relevance for me. My art is different from your own. It consists not in defeating others, but of not being defeated."

The samurai scratched his head and asked," But what school do you belong to, then?"

"It's the school of unarmed combat."

"If that's the case then why do you carry two swords."

"This forces me to retain my self-mastery and not respond to challenges. It's a sacred vow."

In exasperation the samurai continued," And you really think that you can fight me without a sword?"

"Why not? There's even the possibility that I will win!"

Losing his temper, the samurai shouted to the oarsman to take them to the nearest bank, but Bokuden suggested it would be better to land on an island, far from any houses, so as not to draw a crowd, and to be left alone. The samurai accepted. When the raft touched the shore of an uninhabited island, the samurai jumped ashore and drew his sword, ready for combat.

Bokuden carefully took off his two swords and gave them to the oarsman for safekeeping. He then made as if to jump to the ground, but suddenly grabbed the boatman's pole and swiftly pushed the raft back into the current away from the shore.

Bokuden then looked back at the samurai, who was gesticulating wildly on this desert island, and yelled, "See, that's all there is to winning without weapons!"

### Three Flies

A samurai sat alone at his table in a remote inn. Despite the three flies buzzing around him, he radiated a sense of extraordinary calm.

Three *ronin* (masterless samurai) entered the inn. Their envy was excited by the magnificent pair of swords they saw the lone samurai carrying. Confident—they were three against one—they sat at a neighboring table and began trying to provoke the samurai. He remained imperturbable, as if he had not noticed the three *ronin*. Far from being discouraged they became even more derisive. All at once, the samurai caught the three flies buzzing around him with three rapid movements of the chopsticks he was holding in his hand. Then he calmly set the chopsticks back down, completely indifferent to the alarm his gesture had caused among his neighbors. In fact, not only did they shut up but they immediately took to their heels in flight. They had just realized they had tried to pick a fight with someone of formidable mastery. It was only later that they learned, to their terror, that the man who had so easily discouraged their belligerent intentions was the famous master Miyamoto Musashi.

### The Disarmed Assassin

Lord Tayko studied *cha no yu,* the tea ceremony, with Sen no Rikyu, a master of extremely great poise and serenity. Kato, a samurai in Tayko's retinue, regarded his lord's passion for the tea ceremony with a jaundiced eye because he felt it was a waste of time and detrimental to affairs of state. An idea gradually occurred to him: just simply do away with Sen no Rikyu. In order to execute his plan Kato arranged for the tea master to invite him to come drink a cup of tea in his company.

Sen no Rikyu, who, thanks to his art, had attained a very high level of inner awareness, guessed the samurai's criminal intentions at first glance.

"Leave your sword by the door. You will have no need of it in a peaceful tea ceremony," the master explained.

"A samurai is never parted from his sword, no matter what the circumstances," Kato replied.

"Very well, keep your sword and come in for a cup of tea," the Master responded.

The two men sat facing one another and Kato set his sword down within hand's reach. Sen no Rikyu began preparing the tea. Suddenly he overturned the pot that was sitting over the fire. The room filled with steam, smoke, and cinders, accompanied by an atrocious whistling noise. In a panic, the samurai fled outdoors. The tea master apologized for the mishap, "It's all my fault. Please come back in for a cup of tea. I am holding your sword that is covered with ashes. I will clean it and return it to you." The samurai then realized that it would be extremely difficult to kill the tea master, and he abandoned his scheme.

### A Convincing Demonstration

A *ronin* paid a visit to the illustrious master of the art of the sword, Matajuro Yagyu, to see for himself if the latter's reputation had not been not exaggerated.

Master Yagyu tried to explain to the *ronin* that he found the motive of his visit stupid and that he saw no earthly reason for accepting his challenge. But the visitor, who had the air of being a formidable expert himself, and was avidly seeking celebrity, had decided to push the matter to its limits and, in order to provoke the master, didn't hesitate to call him a coward.

This had no apparent effect on Matajuro Yagyu's air of tranquility, but he signaled the *ronin* with his fingers to follow him into the garden. He next pointed with his finger to the top of a tree. Was this a ruse for diverting the *ronin*'s attention? The visitor placed his hand on his sword hilt and retreated several steps before casting a glance in the direction indicated. Two birds were clearly visible there, perched on a branch. What happened then?

Without taking his eyes off them, Master Yagyu took in a deep breath that he only released in the form of a *kiai*, a formidable shout of power. Thunderstruck, the two birds fell to the ground where they lay motionless.

"What do you think of that?" the master asked his guest.

"In- . . . credible . . ." the *ronin* stammered, obviously as shaken as if he had been transfixed by the *kiai* as well.

"But you haven't seen anything yet." the master continued.

Master Yagyu's second *kiai* then echoed through the garden. This time the birds beat their wings and took flight.

So did the *ronin*.

## The Heart of the Willow

The doctor Shirobei Akyama had gone to China to study medicine, acupuncture, and several holds in *shuai chiao*, Chinese wrestling.

On his return to Japan he settled near Nagasaki and began to teach what he had learned. To combat illnesses he employed potent remedies. In his wrestling practice he used much of his strength. But before an illness that was too delicate or too strong, his remedies were useless. Against an adversary who was too strong, his techniques remained ineffective. One by one his students abandoned him. Discouraged, Shirobei started questioning the principles of his method. In order to see the matter with more clarity, he decided to retire to a small temple and impose upon himself a meditation of one hundred days.

During the many hours of meditation he continually bumped up against the same question: Opposing strength with strength is not a solution because a given amount of strength will always be bested by a greater amount of strength. So, what should I do?" he asked himself.

One morning during a snowstorm while he was walking in the garden of the temple, he received his long-sought answer. After hearing the air punctuated by the snapping sound of the branches of a cherry tree breaking under the weight of the snow, he spied a willow tree on the banks of the river.

The supple branches of the willow would sag under the weight of the snow until they were freed of their burden. They would then return to their original position intact.

This vision illuminated Shirobei. He rediscovered the great principles of the Tao. The phrases of Lao-tsu ran through his mind:

*He who bends will rise back up,*
*She who bows remains whole.*

*Nothing is softer and more yielding than water.*
*But to vanquish the rigid and unyielding,*
*Nothing surpasses it.*

*Rigidity is the corridor to death;*
*Flexibility is the corridor to life.*

The Nagasaki doctor completely reformulated his teaching, which then took the name of Yoshinryu, the school of the heart of the willow, the art of flexibility. And he taught this to countless students.

## Letting the Rooster Mature

The king of Chû had entrusted to Chi Hsing Tseu the raising of a promising fighting rooster, who appeared both skilled
and combative. The king was therefore well within his rights
to expect the bird to be quickly broken in and trained, so he
did not understand why he still had not received any word
on the fowl's development ten days after training had begun. He decided to go find Chi in person to ask if the rooster
was ready.

"Oh, no, sire, he is far from being mature enough. He is
still too proud and irritable," Chi answered.

Another ten days went by. The king, impatient, went for
more news to Chi, who answered, "The rooster is making
progress but he is not yet ready because he still reacts as
soon as he senses the presence of another rooster."

Ten days later, the king, now very irritated at having had
to wait so long, came to pick up the rooster for a match. Chi
interposed himself between the king and his bird, explaining, "Not yet, it is way too soon! Your rooster hasn't totally
lost his desire to fight and his hotheaded nature is always
waiting for a pretext to manifest itself."

The king didn't really understand what old Chi was prat-
tling on about. Weren't vitality and high spirits guarantees
for a bird's effectiveness as a fighter? But because Chi Hsing

Tseu was the most reputable trainer in the entire kingdom, the king gave him his trust and waited.

Another ten days went past. The sovereign's patience had reached its limit. He ordered Chi to be brought before him and greeted him in a tone that revealed the extent of his ill humor. With a smile, Chi spoke up in his defense, "In any case, the rooster is almost ready. Indeed, when he hears other cocks crowing he doesn't even react anymore, he remains indifferent to provocation, staying as still as if he were made of wood. His abilities are now solidly anchored within, and his inner strength is developed to a considerable extent."

In fact, when the king wished to make his rooster fight, the other cocks were obviously no match for him. Furthermore they would not even risk themselves fighting his rooster and would flee as soon as they caught sight of him.

# 8

## The Ultimate Secret

*He who has won the secret of* budo *contains
the very universe within himself and can say:
I am the universe. This is why when someone
attempts to fight me he is actually confronting
the universe itself and his action necessarily
disrupts the balance. But at the very moment
he has the thought of measuring himself
against me, he has already been vanquished.*

**VESHIBA MORIHEI**

As mysterious as their secret may be, the great masters have left significant testimonies about it that are disarming in their simplicity.

"The true target that the archer should aim at is his own heart," is a maxim of *kyudo*, the way of archery. In Japanese *kokoro* means heart, but also mind, and spirit, the individual. As the physical heart is anchored in the body, the *kokoro* is the center of the individual that causes his most profound essence to quiver beneath the shell of appearances.

Like mountain guides, the masters point out the path, the stages through which one must proceed to succeed in aiming at one's own heart. The famous Zen master Takuan taught his no less illustrious disciple Tajima no Kami, the shogun's sword instructor, that the way of the heart begins by the "nondispersion of energy," a true and veritable "concentration." He explains, in fact, that if one's *ki* is guided by the movements of one's adversary, it is hypnotized by them; if it is governed by defense, it is captured by the idea of defense. With the *ki* a prisoner, one is at the mercy of one's opponent. To free it, Takuan recommends that one allow it to fill all of one's body and to let it traverse the totality of one's being. Then, if it is necessary to use one's hands or legs, no time or energy will be wasted. The response adapted to circumstances will be as instantaneous and immediate as a spark. If *ki*'s fluidity is preserved by keeping it free of mental deliberations and emotional reactions, it will act wherever necessary and with all the speed of a stroke of lightning.

The Japanese call this fluidity of *ki*, *munen*, or *muso*, that is "nonmental," "non-ego." Japanese tradition compares this state to the clarity of the moon that, although a single object, will be reflected indiscriminately and instantaneously wherever there is water.

Similarly to Master Takuan's advice of letting *ki* fill the entire body, Taoists and tai chi masters state that the human body is like the earth: it possesses underground rivers. "If these rivers are not obstructed, energy will flow naturally." This body wisdom seems to have been forgotten by many contemporary experts who confuse "mastery of the body" with overdeveloped muscles, increased stamina, and building oneself a "record-breaking" physique." Taoist adepts didn't let down their guard, however: "A practitioner of the Tao maintains his physical body with the same pains he would take in caring for a precious stone, because without the body, the Tao cannot be attained."

In fact, the way of the martial arts rests entirely on working with the body, meditating with the body. The body serves as a container for an energy that will open inside and perform a mysterious kind of alchemy.

"If the adept balances the small universe that is his body, he will then be in harmony with the cosmos," the Taoists say. "The way of the martial arts is to make the heart of the universe one's own heart, which simply means making oneself one with the universe." This profound statement comes from Master Ueshiba.

Esoteric science, like all the great traditions, teaches that man is a microcosm, that is to say, a smaller model of the macrocosm, the universe. The human being contains in a latent state all the dimensions of the universe; he obeys the same laws and follows the same rhythms. The art of aiming at one's own heart will lead to a balanced state whose purpose is "plugging into" the source of the original *ki*. It is said that the great masters have torn away the suffocating screen of the ego in order to allow the breath of the universe to traverse their being. Through *wu-wei* (nonresistance) they have mastered "the art without artifice."

"When a master goes by, the dogs don't bark," is a common Eastern saying. Reconciled with himself and the universe, "he absorbs the other into his own heart," Master Ueshiba confides to us. The presence of such an individual balances all that surrounds him.

"With one end of his bow, the archer pierces heaven, with the other, earth, and the bowstring that connects them hurls the arrow at the heart of both the visible and the invisible target." The archer is the true man, the one who, according to the book of Chinese rituals, plays a role in creation, along with earth and heaven: "Heaven engenders, earth nurtures, and man achieves." The man who practices the art of aiming at his own heart finds his true place in the union between mind and body, heaven and earth.

The way of the martial arts, such as it is taught by the rare, authentic masters, and which should not be confused with its imitations, is an Ariadne's thread that can lead us to the key that will allow us to meet the challenges it lays out.

In any event, the masters insist that whatever way is chosen to help resolve the enigma posed by the universe and by our own lives, the great adventure is only possible as lived experience, at the cost of an intensive apprenticeship under the direction of a true master. But it is necessary to realize, they add, that the ultimate reality cannot be communicated by words or symbols. An experienced guide can give advice and encouragement, but the secret cannot be transmitted from one man to another—it must be won.

*Whatever you learn*
*listening to the words of others*
*is forgotten quite quickly"*

## FUNAKOSHI GISHIN

*To know something means having*
*experienced it concretely. A cookbook*
*will not take away your hunger"*

## TAKUAN

### The Look of Disillusionment

In the Okinawan capital of Naha, an artisan earned his living carving objects that people brought to his shop. Though over forty years old, he maintained a powerful musculature that gave him a formidable appearance.

One day, a man who did not appear to be any more than thirty entered the shop to order a carving. He was a large man with a proud bearing, but it was the strangeness of his eyes that commanded attention. On this day, however, his gaze, hypnotic as that of an eagle, was filled with a deep bitterness.

The artisan did not hesitate to ask, "Pardon my curiosity, sir, but aren't you Matsumura, the famous karate instructor?"

"Yes, I am, actually. What of it?"

"I knew it!" the carver exclaimed. "You know I've been

wanting to take karate lessons from you for as long as I can remember."

"Impossible, I no longer teach. I don't even want to hear the word karate anymore," was Matsumura's astounding reply to this statement.

"I don't understand, aren't you the clan leader's personal karate teacher?"

"I was. It is in fact the clan leader himself who has chased away any desire I ever had to teach karate."

"You are one of the best teachers in the country. I don't see what you mean"

"Well the answer is simple enough. The clan leader has enormous flaws in his karate practice. He is too vain to acknowledge them, and he is too careless to make the effort necessary to correct them. I am no longer sure how to deal with the man. During our last session, I asked him to attack me so that I could correct the faults in his attack. He went on the offensive with a leaping kick, a mistake even the greenest of beginners wouldn't make. I chopped him down in mid air with a *shuto* (an openhanded punch) and he sprawled out on the floor, half stunned. That's how I lost my position."

"I see . . . but you shouldn't make such a big deal about it, he will surely hire you back again. He can't easily find a better teacher than you."

"I don't think he will ever forgive me. But that's beside the point, in any case, as I've decided to give up teaching."

"That's stupid. You should realize life has lots of ups and

downs. Besides which, I'm still totally determined to take lessons from you."

"Don't count on it," Matsumura dryly interjected, "anyway, an expert such as yourself has nothing to learn from me."

The carver was also a highly esteemed expert in his field.

"How would you know?" the carver persisted, "you probably have a lot you can teach me."

"You're really starting to get on my nerves!" Matsumura yelled back.

"If you insist on refusing to give me a lesson then you must grant me a match with you," the artisan suggested.

"What! Are you feeling all right? You're not making any sense."

"Don't tell me you are scared! Of course forcing to make me eat dirt won't be as easy for you as it was with the clan leader!"

"You look strong enough, but don't you think you might be playing a dangerous game! Have you really given any thought to the risks of a combat that takes place between life and death? You must certainly know the old proverb that says when two tigers fight, one will be wounded and the other killed."

"I will accept that risk. And you?"

"Whenever you like," Matsumura answered.

The next morning at the first glimmer of dawn, the two men met each other in an isolated field. The carver adopted a defensive posture that left no opening available. In contrast,

Matsumura took a natural position *(shizen tai)*, with his arms dangling loosely at his side. Had he gone crazy to take such a vulnerable stance? This thought flashed briefly through the carver's mind as he prepared to strike the first blow. He cautiously and carefully approached his opponent, who did not move even an inch. Suddenly, at the very moment the carver prepared to leap, he fell over backwards as if pushed back by some terrible force.

Matsumura, however, hadn't even made the slightest gesture. He remained in the same position with his arms dangling loosely at his side.

Beads of sweat pearled up on the carver's forehead, while he lifted his now pale head and attempted to regain his feet. What had just happened to him? He appeared to have been knocked to the ground by the unbearable look Matsumura had hurled at him, a look that had stricken him to his very depths. Was such a thing possible? But the poor artisan didn't keep worrying about it; he couldn't quit, his honor was at stake. He therefore put his guard back up and moved forward. He had hardly taken a few steps when he stopped, incapable of advancing any further. He felt hypnotized by Matsumura's gaze, as if he were caught in a trap and emptied of all substance.

Incapable of taking his eyes from those of his adversary, the carver made a supreme effort to break the spell. With all his remaining strength he let out a *kiai,* but to no effect. Matsumura did not even blink. In desperation, the carver lowered his guard and began retreating.

"Now would be the time to go on the offensive, by some means other than yelling," Matsumura told him with a smile.

"This is incredible. This is beyond me. I, who have never lost a single combat . . . but too bad for me, I have to end this," the artisan murmured to himself before launching a suicidal attack. He didn't even have the time to execute his movement; he was stopped midstride by a *kiai* from Matsumura, a fantastic shout that came from the very depths of his being, a cry from another world.

Lying on the ground as if paralyzed, the carver stammered the same words several times before he managed to make himself understood, "I quit, I quit." The artisan then painfully turned his head to look at his vanquisher and said to him piteously, "What a lunatic I was to try to provoke you. The level I've reached in my training is ridiculous next to yours."

"I don't agree," Matsumura responded, "I am sure you have achieved an excellent level of skill. In other conditions, I fear that I would have been defeated."

"Don't try and console me. I have lost all my strength only from feeling your gaze transfix me."

"That's possible," Matsumura said, going on to explain, "but I believe the reason is the following: You were merely determined to win. I was quite determined to die if I lost. That is the sole difference between us. Yesterday, when I entered your shop, I was completely absorbed by my own sorrows and my troubles with the clan leader. Those little annoyances evaporated when you provoked me. I realized they were simply details of no importance. Your challenge fixed my gaze back upon the essential."

~~~~~

## The Teachings of the Venerable Cat

This strange tale is taken from an old book on the art of the sword, probably written by a seventeenth-century master of the Ittoryu school. A "philosophical tale" of Taoist and Zen inspiration, it contains essential information on the secret of the martial arts.

Shoken, an expert in the art of swordsmanship, had been plagued for several days by a rat who had moved into his house. The best cats from the surrounding area had been brought into the house, which had been transformed into a sort of arena for the occasion. To the surprise of everyone, these matches always ended with the same scenario: the hunter, terrified by the attacks of the rat, would flee the battlefield meowing piteously.

In desperation, the expert decided to take on the task of killing this terrible beast himself. Armed with his sword, Shoken went on the offensive. But fast as lightning, the rat dodged all of his blows. Shoken intensified his efforts. The rat remained untouchable. Covered in sweat and out of breath, the expert finally gave up. Would he now be forced to give up half his house to this cursed rat? He found this prospect making him increasingly depressed.

One day, he heard talk of a cat with a reputation as the greatest rat hunter in the province. When Shoken saw the famous cat, all remaining hope left him. The elderly animal was truly nothing to look at. Having nothing to lose, however, he brought the cat home and let it into the room where the rat held sway. The cat entered the room, treading serenely, as if nothing were amiss. When the rat saw him, it froze where it stood, clearly terrified. The cat calmly approached it, caught it with no effort, and left the room, holding its prey in its mouth.

That evening, all the cats that had taken part in the rat hunt gathered together at Shoken's house. The great cat, as the hero of the day, was respectfully invited to take the place of honor. One of the other cats took the floor, "We are considered the most experienced cats in the village. But not one of us managed to do what you have done with that terrible rat. Your mastery is truly extraordinary. We are burning with impatience to know your secret."

The venerable cat responded, "Before trying to impart to you the principles of the Great Art, the direction of the way, I would like to hear what you have learned and how you were trained."

The black cat rose up and said, "Born into a famous family of rat hunters, I was trained from infancy in this art. I am capable of making leaps of six feet, and insinuating myself into rat holes, in short, I have become an expert in all manner of acrobatics. On the other hand, I know a great number of ruses and have more than one trick up my sleeve. I am ashamed at having had to beat a retreat before that old rat."

The great cat explained, "You have only learned technique. You are only concerned with knowing how to plan out your attack. The ancients have in fact invented techniques with the sole aim of initiating us into the most appropriate method for performing a task. The method is naturally simple and efficacious. It contains all the essential aspects of the art. Technical prowess is not the goal of the art. It is merely a means that must remain in accord with the way. If the way is neglected and efficiency trumps it in importance, the art of combat will quickly degenerate and be used for any conceivable purpose. Never forget this."

The tiger cat stepped forward to proffer his advice. "In my opinion the most important thing in the art of combat is *ki*, energy, the mind. I have trained long to develop it. I now possess the most powerful mind around, one capable of filling heaven and earth. Once I have confronted an adversary, my *ki* imposes itself upon him and my victory is assured even before the fight actually begins. Even when a rat is running across a roof beam I can catch him, all I need do is direct my *ki* at him to make him fall. But with this mysterious rat, nothing worked. It was beyond me.

The venerable cat replied, "You are capable of utilizing a large portion of your psychic powers, but the simple fact that you are aware of your ability to do so works against you. Opposing an adversary with your potent psychic strength is not a solution because you always run the risk of encountering someone stronger than you. You say that your mind fills heaven and earth, but you are mistaken. It is not actually your mind itself but only its shadow. You should never confuse psychic power with the mind. True mind is a wave of inexhaustible energy that flows like a river, whereas your force depends on certain conditions much like those torrents that only exist during a storm. This difference in origin necessarily entails a difference in results. A cornered rat often shows itself to be more combative than the cat attacking it. It is on the alert and its entire being embodies the very spirit of combat. It is the rare cat that even has a chance of breaking down its resistance."

The gray cat then took the floor. "As you have just finished saying, spirit is always accompanied by its shadow, and no matter how strong it is, an enemy can take advantage of this shadow. I have trained for a long time not to resist the enemy, but, on the contrary, to seek to use his own strength against him. Thanks to my flexibility, even the most powerful rats can't manage to strike me. But this astounding rat wasn't caught in the snare of my attitude of nonresistance."

The old cat responded, "What you call the attitude of nonresistance is not in harmony with nature. It is actually a gimmick fabricated by your intellect. Artificial nonresistance requires a psychic will that interferes with the quality of your perceptions and obstructs the spontaneity of your movements. In order to allow nature to manifest thoroughly, it is necessary to rid yourself of all mental constraints. When nature follows its own path and acts as it pleases within you, there is no longer any shadow or any fault from which your adversary can profit.

"Although I am but a simple cat who doesn't have a great knowledge of human affairs, allow me to bring up the art of the sword to express a deeper truth. The art of the sword doesn't consist merely in vanquishing one's adversary. It is primarily the art of being aware, at a critical moment, of the cause of life and death. A samurai must keep this in mind and strive for spiritual training as well as knowledge of fighting techniques. Therefore, he must attempt to penetrate into the cause of life and death. When he has attained this level of being, he is free of all egotistical thought, nourishes no negative emotion, and doesn't waste time in calculations and deliberations. His mind is then nonresistant and in harmony with all that surrounds him.

"When you have succeeded in achieving the state of nondesire, your mind, which by nature is formless, contains no object. The spiritual energy *ki* will then expand in a balanced manner with no blockages. If, on the other hand, an object attracts it, the energy seesaws and flows in a single direction, leaving a void in the other. Where there is too much, it will overflow and be out of control. The place where *ki* is lacking will not be sufficiently nourished and will begin to shrivel up. In both cases you will find yourself incapable of confronting situations that are constantly changing. But when nondesire has prevailed, the mind is not drawn in any single direction, and it transcends both subject and object."

Shoken then asked the question, "What do you mean when you say 'it transcends the subject and the object'?"

The venerable cat stated, "Because there is an ego, there is also an enemy. When the ego no longer exists, there is no more enemy. If you stick a word on things, if you enclose things in fixed and artificial forms, they appear to exist in opposition. Male opposes female, fire opposes water. But when there is no judgment within your mind, no conflict of opposites can take place. There is then no longer either an ego or an enemy. When the intellect has been surpassed, you get a taste of the state of absolute 'nonaction,' you are in serene harmony with the universe. You no longer have to choose between true or false, pleasing or displeasing. You are free of the dualistic world manufactured by your intellect. But when even an extremely tiny piece of dust enters our eyes, we can no longer keep them open. The mind is similar to the eye; once an object has entered it, its power is spent.

"This is all I can explain to you here on this matter. It's up to you to experience its truth. True understanding is found outside of all written teachings. A special transmission from one man to another is necessary, but in any event the truth is only obtained by one's own efforts. Teaching is not difficult, nor is listening; what is truly difficult is to become conscious of who you really are inside. *Satori,* awakening, is nothing other than the fact of truly seeing within yourself. *Satori* is the end of a dream. Awakening, self-realization, and seeing within yourself are no more and no less than synonyms."